Tolley's
Capital Gains Tax
Workbook
2006/07

by

Kevin Walton BA (Hons)
Andrew Flint MA CTA

LexisNexis®
Tolley

Members of the LexisNexis Group worldwide

United Kingdom	LexisNexis Butterworths, a Division of Reed Elsevier (UK) Ltd, Halsbury House, 35 Chancery Lane, LONDON, WC2A 1EL, and RSH, 1–3 Baxter's Place, Leith Walk, EDINBURGH EH1 3AF
Argentina	LexisNexis Argentina, BUENOS AIRES
Australia	LexisNexis Butterworths, CHATSWOOD, New South Wales
Austria	LexisNexis Verlag ARD Orac GmbH & Co KG, VIENNA
Benelux	LexisNexis Benelux, AMSTERDAM
Canada	LexisNexis Butterworths, MARKHAM, Ontario
Chile	LexisNexis Chile Ltda, SANTIAGO
China	LexisNexis China, BEIJING AND SHANGHAI
France	LexisNexis SA, PARIS
Germany	LexisNexis Deutschland GmbH, MUNSTER
Hong Kong	LexisNexis, HONG KONG
India	LexisNexis India, NEW DELHI
Italy	Giuffrè Editore, MILAN
Japan	LexisNexis Japan, TOKYO
Malaysia	Malayan Law Journal Sdn Bhd, KUALA LUMPUR
Mexico	LexisNexis Mexico, MEXICO
New Zealand	LexisNexis NZ Ltd, WELLINGTON
Poland	Wydawnictwo Prawnicze LexisNexis Sp, WARSAW
Singapore	LexisNexis Singapore, SINGAPORE
South Africa	LexisNexis Butterworths, DURBAN
USA	LexisNexis, DAYTON, Ohio

© Reed Elsevier (UK) Ltd 2006

Published by LexisNexis Butterworths

A CIP Catalogue record for this book is available from the British Library.

ISBN 10: 0 7545 3053 1
ISBN 13: 9780 7545 3053 4

Typeset by Interactive Sciences Ltd, Gloucester
Printed in Great Britain by Hobbs the Printers Ltd, Totton, Hampshire

Visit LexisNexis Butterworths at www.lexisnexis.co.uk

About This Book

Tolley's Capital Gains Tax Workbook illustrates the practical application of UK capital gains tax and corporation tax on chargeable gains legislation through worked examples. The computations aid understanding of complex areas of the law and provide guidance on layout. Detailed explanatory notes and statutory references are provided wherever appropriate. The comprehensive index and table of statutes make it easy to find a particular computation quickly.

The Workbook is designed to be used on its own or in conjunction with Tolley's Capital Gains Tax, and so the chapters follow the order of the commentary in that volume.

This 2006/07 edition is fully up to date and includes the provisions of Finance Act 2006. Cross-references prefixed 'IT' and 'CT' refer to the companion volumes Tolley's Income Tax Workbook 2006/07 and Tolley's Corporation Tax Workbook 2006/07.

Comments and suggestions for improvements are always welcome.

Abbreviations and References

ABBREVIATIONS

ACT	=	Advance Corporation Tax
Art	=	Article
b/f	=	brought forward
C/A	=	Court of Appeal
CCAB	=	Consultative Committee of Accountancy Bodies
C/D	=	Chancery Division
c/f	=	carried forward
CGT	=	Capital Gains Tax
CGTA	=	Capitals Gains Tax Act 1979
CT	=	Corporation Tax
DTR	=	Double Tax Relief
EIS	=	Enterprise Investment Scheme
ESC	=	Extra-Statutory Concession
FA	=	Finance Act
F(No 2)A	=	Finance (No 2) Act
FIFO	=	First In, First Out
FYA	=	First-Year Allowance
H/L	=	House of Lords
HMIT	=	Her Majesty's Inspector of Taxes
ICTA	=	Income and Corporation Taxes Act 1988
IRPR	=	Inland Revenue Press Release
IT	=	Income Tax
ITEPA	=	Income Tax (Earnings and Pensions) Act
ITTOIA	=	Income Tax (Trading and Other Income) Act
LIFO	=	Last In, First Out
NBV	=	Net Book Value
para	=	paragraph
PAYE	=	Pay As You Earn
P/e	=	Period ended
Reg	=	Regulation
s	=	section
SC/S	=	Scottish Court of Session
Sch	=	Schedule
Sec	=	Section
SI	=	Statutory Instrument
SSAP	=	Statement of Standard Accounting Practice
TCGA	=	Taxation of Chargeable Gains Act 1992
TMA	=	Taxes Management Act 1970
Y/e	=	Year ended

REFERENCES

STC	=	Simon's Tax Cases, (LexisNexis Butterworths, Halsbury House, 35 Chancery Lane, London, WC2A 1EL)
TC	=	Official Tax Cases (H.M. Stationery Office, P.O. Box 276, SW8 5DT)

Contents

CHAPTER		PAGE
201	Annual Rates and Exemptions	2
202	Anti-Avoidance	5
203	Assets	10
204	Assets held on 6 April 1965	12
205	Assets held on 31 March 1982	28
206	Capital Sums derived from Assets	34
207	Companies	40
208	Computation of Gains and Losses	43
209	Enterprise Investment Scheme	48
210	Exemptions and Reliefs	53
211	Hold-Over Reliefs	56
212	Indexation	62
213	Interest on Overpaid Tax	70
214	Interest and Surcharges on Unpaid Tax	71
215	Land	72
216	Losses	85
217	Married Persons and Civil Partners	91
218	Mineral Royalties	94
219	Offshore Settlements	96
220	Overseas Matters	102
221	Partnerships	107
222	Private Residences	114
223	Qualifying Corporate Bonds	120
224	Rollover Relief — Replacement of Business Assets	123
225	Settlements	130
226	Shares and Securities	138
227	Shares and Securities — Identification Rules	158
228	Taper Relief	164
229	Wasting Assets	172
	Table of Statutes	175
	Index	180

201   Annual Rates and Exemptions

201.1 **GAINS CHARGEABLE AT INCOME TAX RATES** [*TCGA 1992, s 4; FA 2000, s 37*]

M, a single person and established sole trader, had trading income of £15,000 for the year ended 30 April 2006, but made a trading loss of £11,000 for the year ended 30 April 2007. He had no other source of income, but realised a capital gain (after taper relief) of £42,900 in 2006/07 from the sale of a country cottage. He claims relief for the trading loss under *ICTA 1988, s 380(1)(b)* against his income for 2006/07.

M's income tax position for 2006/07 is as follows

	£
Trading income	15,000
Less: Loss relief	11,000
	4,000
Less: Personal allowance (maximum £5,035)	4,000
Taxable income	Nil

His capital gains tax computation is as follows

	£
Gain	42,900
Annual exemption	8,800
Gain chargeable to tax	£34,100

Capital gains tax payable	£
2,150 at 10%	215.00
31,150 at 20%	6,230.00
800 at 40%	320.00
£34,100	£6,765.00

Notes

(a)   An individual's gains are chargeable at a rate equivalent to the lower rate of income tax (20%). However, to the extent if any that gains, if treated as the top slice of income, exceed the basic rate limit (£33,300 for 2006/07), they are chargeable at 40%. The 10% starting rate of income tax also applies to gains to the extent that, again if treated as though they were the top slice of taxable income, they fall within the starting rate band (£2,150 for 2006/07).

(b)   The unused personal allowance of £1,035 is not available to reduce the chargeable gain. If M's trading losses had exceeded his total income, he could have claimed, under *FA 1991, s 72*, to have the gain reduced by the unused losses (see IT 13.2 LOSSES).

201.2 **ANNUAL EXEMPTION** [*TCGA 1992, s 2(2)(4)–(8), s 3; FA 2002, s 51, Sch 11 paras 2, 7, 8*]

(A) Interaction with losses

For 2006/07, R has chargeable gains (after indexation but before taper relief) of £15,800 and allowable losses of £4,000. He also has allowable losses of £12,000 brought forward.

	£
Adjusted net gains (£15,800 − £4,000)	11,800
Losses brought forward (part)	3,000
	8,800
Annual exempt amount	8,800
Taxable gains	Nil
Losses brought forward	12,000
Less utilised in 2006/07	3,000
Losses carried forward	£9,000

Note

(*a*)   TAPER RELIEF (228), if otherwise available in respect of the 2006/07 chargeable gains, is effectively lost as the taxable gains are reduced to nil in any case.

(B) Interaction with losses and settlement gains attributed under *TCGA 1992, s 87*

(i)

For 2006/07, P has the same gains and losses (including brought-forward losses) as R above, but is also a beneficiary of an offshore trust. Trust gains of £9,200 are attributed to her for 2006/07 under *TCGA 1992, s 87*.

	£
Adjusted net gains (£15,800 − £4,000 + £8,800 (note (*a*))	20,600
Losses brought forward (part)	11,800
	8,800
Annual exempt amount	8,800
	Nil
Add: section 87 gains not brought in above	400
Taxable gains	£400
Losses brought forward	12,000
Less utilised in 2006/07	11,800
Losses carried forward	£200

(ii)

Q is in the same position as P except that his attributed gains are only £6,300.

	£
Adjusted net gains (£15,800 − £4,000 + £6,300)	18,100
Losses brought forward (part)	9,300
	8,800
Annual exempt amount	8,800
Taxable gains	Nil
Losses brought forward	12,000
Less utilised in 2006/07	9,300
Losses carried forward	£2,700

Notes

(a)   Attributed gains (as in (b) below) are included in adjusted net gains *only* to the extent that they do not exceed the annual exempt amount. Such gains cannot be covered by personal losses and will already have been reduced by any taper relief available to the trustees. The exempt amount is effectively allocated to attributed gains in priority to personal gains.

(b)   For the purposes of (a) above, 'attributed gains' include non-resident settlement gains attributed to a beneficiary under *TCGA 1992, s 87* (as in this example) and those similarly attributed under *TCGA 1992, s 89(2)*. For years before 2003/04, unless, in relation to gains accruing in any one or more of the years 2000/01 to 2002/03 inclusive, an election is made under *FA 2002, Sch 11 para 8* to enable the set-off of personal losses against them (see 216.2 LOSSES), 'attributed gains' also include gains charged on a settlor under *TCGA 1992, s 77* (UK settlement) or *s 86* (non-resident settlement).

202   Anti-Avoidance

202.1 VALUE SHIFTING [*TCGA 1992, s 29*]

Jak owns all the 1,000 £1 ordinary shares of K Ltd. The shares were acquired on subscription in 1978 for £1,000 and had a value of £65,250 on 31 March 1982. In December 2006, the trustees of Jak's family settlement subscribed at par for 250 £1 ordinary shares in K Ltd, thereby acquiring 20% of the voting power in the company.

It is agreed that the value per share of Jak's holding immediately before the December 2006 share issue was £175 and immediately afterwards was £150. The value per share of the trust's holding, on issue, was £97 per share.

The proceeds of the deemed disposal are computed as follows

Value passing out of Jak's 1,000 shares is £25,000 (1,000 × £25 per share (£175 − £150)).

Value passing into the trust's 250 shares is £24,250 (250 × £97 per share) *less* the subscription price paid of £250 (250 × £1 per share) = £24,000.

The proceeds of the deemed disposal are equal to the value passing into the new shares, i.e. £24,000. (The trust's acquisition cost is £24,250, i.e. actual plus deemed consideration given.)

The disposal is a part disposal (see 208.2 COMPUTATION OF GAINS AND LOSSES), the value of the part retained being £150,000 (1,000 × £150 per share).

Jak will have a capital gain for 2006/07 as follows (subject to indexation allowance to April 1998 and TAPER RELIEF (228))

	£
Proceeds of deemed disposal	24,000
Allowable cost $\dfrac{24,000}{24,000 + 150,000} \times £65,250$	9,000
Unindexed gain	£15,000

Note

(*a*)   The legislation taxes the amount of value passing *into* the transferee holdings, not (if different) the amount passing from the transferor. The deemed proceeds are thus equal to the value received by the transferee(s). See HMRC Capital Gains Manual CG 58855.

202.2 VALUE-SHIFTING TO GIVE TAX-FREE BENEFIT [*TCGA 1992, s 30, Sch 11 para 10(1)*]

M owns the whole of the issued share capital in C Ltd, an unquoted company. He is also a director of the company. M receives an offer from a public company for his shares. Prior to sale, C Ltd pays M £30,000 for loss of his office as director. M then sells the shares for £100,000.

On the sale of M's shares, HMRC may seek to adjust the consideration in computing M's chargeable gain on the grounds that M has received a tax-free benefit and the value of his shares has thereby been materially reduced.

202.3 VALUE SHIFTING: DISTRIBUTION WITHIN A GROUP FOLLOWED BY A DISPOSAL OF SHARES [*TCGA 1992, ss 30, 31, Sch 11 para 10(2)*]

Topco Ltd owns 100% of A Ltd, which owns 100% of B Ltd. Both A and B were acquired for negligible amounts. A bought some land in 1992 for a relatively small sum. It is now worth £100,000. In an attempt to realise the proceeds of the land at a tax saving, Topco arranges for B to borrow £100,000. In June 2006, A sells the land to B for this amount, and A, which previously had no undistributed reserves, then pays a dividend of £100,000 to Topco. Topco then sells all of its shares in A Ltd to an unconnected person at their market value which is now a nominal sum.

On the sale of the A Ltd shares, HMRC may seek to apply *TCGA 1992, ss 30, 31* to increase the consideration on the sale by Topco Ltd to £100,000.

202.4 ASSETS DISPOSED OF IN A SERIES OF TRANSACTIONS [*TCGA 1992, ss 19, 20*]

L purchased a set of 6 antique chairs in June 1991 at a cost of £12,000. He gave 2 chairs to his daughter in February 2001, another pair to his son in November 2003, and sold the final pair to his brother for their market value in August 2006.

The market value of the chairs at the relevant dates were

	2 chairs £	4 chairs £	6 chairs £
February 2001	6,000	14,000	26,000
November 2003	7,800	18,000	34,200
August 2006	10,400	24,000	46,200

The indexation factor for June 1991 to April 1998 is 0.213.

The capital gains tax computations are as follows

February 2001
Disposal to daughter

Deemed consideration   £6,000

As the consideration does not exceed £6,000, the disposal is covered by the chattel exemption (see note (*a*)).

November 2003
(i)   *2000/01 disposal to daughter recomputed*

Original market value (deemed disposal consideration at
February 2001)   £6,000

Reasonable proportion of aggregate market value as at
February 2001 of all assets disposed of to date
£14,000 × $\frac{2}{4}$ £7,000

	£
Deemed consideration (greater of £6,000 and £7,000)	7,000

$$\text{Cost } \frac{7,000}{7,000 + 14,000} \times £12,000 \qquad\qquad 4,000$$

Unindexed gain	3,000
Indexation allowance £4,000 × 0.213	852
Chargeable gain 2000/01 (subject to TAPER RELIEF (228))	£2,148

(ii) *2003/04 disposal to son*

Original market value (deemed disposal consideration)	£7,800
Reasonable proportion of aggregate market value as at November 2003 of all assets disposed of to date £18,000 × $\frac{2}{4}$	£9,000

	£
Deemed consideration (greater of £7,800 and £9,000)	9,000

$$\text{Cost} \frac{9,000}{9,000 + 7,800} \times (£12,000 - £4,000) \qquad\qquad 4,286$$

Unindexed gain	4,714
Indexation allowance £4,286 × 0.213	913
Chargeable gain 2003/04 (subject to TAPER RELIEF (228))	£3,801

August 2006
(i) *Gain on 2000/01 disposal to daughter recomputed*

Original market value (deemed consideration in recomputation at November 2003)	£7,000
Reasonable proportion of aggregate market value as at February 2001 of all assets disposed of to date £26,000 × $\frac{2}{6}$	£8,667

	£
Deemed consideration (greater of £7,000 and £8,667)	8,667

$$\text{Cost } \frac{8,667}{8,667 + 14,000} \times £12,000 \qquad\qquad 4,588$$

Unindexed gain	4,079
Indexation allowance £4,588 × 0.213	977
Revised chargeable gain 2000/01 (subject to TAPER RELIEF (228))	£3,102

202.4 Anti-Avoidance

(ii) *Gain on 2003/04 disposal to son recomputed*

Original market value (deemed consideration in computation at November 2003)	£9,000
Reasonable proportion of aggregate market value as at November 2003 of all assets disposed of to date £34,200 × $\frac{2}{6}$	£11,400

	£
Deemed consideration (greater of £9,000 and £11,400)	11,400
Cost $\dfrac{11,400}{11,400 + 7,800}$ × (£12,000 − £4,588)	4,401
Unindexed gain	6,999
Indexation allowance £4,401 × 0.213	938
Revised chargeable gain 2003/04 (subject to TAPER RELIEF (228))	£6,061

(iii) *Gain on 2006/07 disposal to brother*

Original market value (actual consideration)	£10,400
Reasonable proportion of aggregate market value as at August 2006 of all assets disposed of to date £46,200 × $\frac{2}{6}$	£15,400

	£
Deemed consideration (greater of £10,400 and £15,400)	15,400
Cost (£12,000 − £4,588 − £4,401)	3,011
Unindexed gain	12,389
Indexation allowance £3,011 × 0.213 (note (*d*))	641
Chargeable gain 2006/07 (subject to TAPER RELIEF (228))	£11,748

Notes

(*a*) The disposal in February 2001 is at first covered by the chattel exemption of £6,000. As the second disposal in November 2003 is to a person connected with the recipient of the first disposal, the two must then be looked at together for the purposes of the chattel exemption, and, as the combined proceeds exceed the chattel exemption limit, the exemption is not available. [*TCGA 1992, s 262*]. See also 210.1(C) EXEMPTIONS AND RELIEFS.

(*b*) The three disposals are linked transactions within *TCGA 1992, s 19* as they are made by the same transferor to persons with whom he is connected, and take place within a six-year period.

(*c*) It is assumed in the above example that it is 'reasonable' to apportion the aggregate market value in proportion to the number of items. In other instances a different basis may be needed to give the 'reasonable' apportionment required by *TCGA 1992, s 20(4)*.

202.5 **DEPRECIATORY TRANSACTIONS: GROUPS OF COMPANIES** [*TCGA 1992, s 176]*

G Ltd owns 100% of the share capital of Q Ltd, which it acquired in June 1989 for £75,000. Q Ltd owns land which it purchased in 1985 for £50,000. In 1998, the land, then with a market value of £120,000, was transferred to G Ltd for £50,000. In April 2006, Q Ltd was put into liquidation, and G Ltd received liquidation distributions totalling £30,000.

The loss on the Q Ltd shares is £45,000 (£75,000 − £30,000). HMRC are likely to disallow the whole or part of the loss on the grounds that it resulted from the depreciatory transaction involving the transfer of land at less than market value.

203   Assets

203.1 **OPTIONS** [*TCGA 1992, ss 44, 46, 144, 144ZA–144ZD, 145; FA 2003, s 158; F(No 2)A 2005, s 35, Sch 5 paras 1, 2, 6*]

Cross-reference. See also 229.2 WASTING ASSETS.

On 1 February 2002 F granted an option to G for £10,000 to acquire freehold land bought by F for £50,000 in September 1995. The option is for a period of 5 years, and the option price is £100,000 plus 1% thereof for each month since the option was granted. On 1 February 2004, G sold the option to H for £20,000. On 30 June 2006, H exercises the option and pays F £141,000 for the land. Neither G nor H intended to use the land for the purposes of a trade.

Indexation factor: September 1995 to April 1998   0.080

2002 Grant of option by F

	£
Disposal proceeds	10,000
Allowable cost	—
Chargeable gain 2001/02 (subject to TAPER RELIEF (228))	£10,000

2004 Disposal of option by G

	£	
Disposal proceeds		20,000
Allowable cost	10,000	
Less: Wasted — £10,000 $\times \frac{2}{5}$	4,000	6,000
Chargeable gain 2003/04		£14,000

2006 Exercise of option

(i) Earlier assessment on F vacated	
(ii) Aggregate disposal proceeds (£10,000 + £141,000)	151,000
Allowable cost of land	50,000
Unindexed gain	101,000
Indexation allowance £50,000 × 0.080	4,000
Chargeable gain (on F) 2006/07 (subject to TAPER RELIEF (228))	£97,000

H's allowable expenditure is

Cost of option (acquired February 2004, so no indexation due)	20,000
Cost of land (acquired June 2006, so no indexation due)	141,000
	£161,000

Notes

(*a*)   The wasting asset rules (see 229 WASTING ASSETS) apply on the disposal of the option by G (though certain options are exempted from these rules — see *TCGA 1992, s 144*). As these rules can only apply on a disposal, they cannot apply on the exercise of the option by H (as the exercise of an option is not treated as a disposal), so his acquisition cost remains intact.

(b)   For the purposes of computing taper relief on a future disposal, H's acquisition of the land is deemed to have occurred on 30 June 2006, i.e. the date he exercised the option and not the date he acquired it. [*TCGA 1992, Sch A1 para 13(3); FA 1998, s 121, Sch 20*].

204   Assets held on 6 April 1965

204.1   **QUOTED SHARES AND SECURITIES** [*TCGA 1992, s 109(4)(5), Sch 2 paras 1–8*]

(A) Basic computation of gain

H acquired 3,000 U plc ordinary shares in 1962 for £15,000. Their market value was £10 per share on 6 April 1965 and £12 per share on 31 March 1982. In September 2006, H sells 2,000 of the shares for £30 per share. The indexation factor for March 1982 to April 1998 is 1.047.

	£	£	£
Sale proceeds	60,000	60,000	60,000
Cost	10,000		
6 April 1965 value		20,000	
31 March 1982 value			24,000
Unindexed gain	50,000	40,000	36,000
Indexation allowance:			
£24,000 × 1.047	25,128	25,128	25,128
Indexed gain	£24,872	£14,872	£10,872
Chargeable gain (subject to TAPER RELIEF (228))			£10,872

Notes

(*a*)   The comparison is firstly between the gain arrived at by deducting cost and that arrived at by deducting 6 April 1965 value. The smaller of the two gains is taken. If, however, an election had been made under either *TCGA 1992, Sch 2 para 4* or *TCGA 1992, s 109(4)* for 6 April 1965 value to be used in computing all gains and losses on quoted shares held at that date, this comparison need not be made and the taxable gain, subject to (*b*) below, would be £14,872.

(*b*)   The second comparison is between the figure arrived at in (*a*) above and the gain using 31 March 1982 value. As the latter is smaller, it is substituted for the figure in (*a*) above by virtue of *TCGA 1992, s 35(2)*. If, however, an election had been made under *TCGA 1992, s 35(5)* for 31 March 1982 value to be used in computing all gains and losses on assets held at that date, neither this comparison nor that in (*a*) above need be made and the taxable gain would still be £10,872.

(*c*)   Indexation is based on 31 March 1982 value in all three calculations as this gives the greater allowance. [*TCGA 1992, s 55(1)(2)*].

(*d*)   All comparisons are between gains *after* indexation and *before* taper relief.

(B) Basic computation—no gain/no loss disposals

J acquired a holding of quoted shares in 1956 for £1,000. The market value of the holding at 6 April 1965 and 31 March 1982 respectively was £19,000 and £20,000. J sells the holding in September 2006 for £18,000. The indexation factor for the period March 1982 to April 1998 is 1.047.

(i) Assuming no elections made to use 1965 value or 1982 value

	£	£
Sale proceeds	18,000	18,000
Cost	1,000	
6 April 1965 value		19,000
Unindexed gain/(loss)	17,000	(1,000)
Indexation allowance:		
£20,000 × 1.047 (see below) = £20,940 but		
restricted to	17,000	—
Indexed gain/(loss)	Nil	£(1,000)
Chargeable gain/allowable loss		Nil

As one computation shows no gain/no loss and the other a loss, the disposal is a no gain/no loss disposal. [*TCGA 1992, Sch 2 para 2(1)*]. There is no need to compute the gain or loss using 31 March 1982 value as re-basing cannot disturb a no gain/no loss position. [*TCGA 1992, s 35(3)(c)*].

(ii) Election made to use 6 April 1965 value

	£	£
Sale proceeds	18,000	18,000
6 April 1965 value	19,000	
31 March 1982 value		20,000
(Loss)	(1,000)	(2,000)
Allowable loss	£1,000	

The allowable loss is £1,000 as re-basing cannot increase a loss. [*TCGA 1992, s 35(3)(b)*].

(iii) Election made to use 31 March 1982 value

There is an allowable loss of £2,000.

13

204.1   Assets held on 6 April 1965

(C) Parts of holding acquired at different times

L has the following transactions in shares of A plc, a quoted company

Date	Number of shares bought/(sold)	Cost/(proceeds) £
9.1.57	1,500	1,050
10.11.62	750	600
15.7.69	1,200	3,000
12.10.80	1,400	5,000
16.12.83	850	5,950
17.9.95	1,150	5,200
19.12.06	(6,000)	(63,000)
	850	

Market value of A shares at 6 April 1965 was £1.60
Market value of A shares at 31 March 1982 was £4.00

Indexation factors	
March 1982 to April 1998 (note (c))	1.047
December 1983 to April 1985	0.091
April 1985 to September 1995	0.589
September 1995 to April 1998 (note (c))	0.080

(i) No election made to substitute 1965 market value

Identify 6,000 shares sold on a LIFO basis as follows

Section 104 holding	Shares	Qualifying Expenditure £	Indexed Pool £
16.12.83 acquisition	850	5,950	5,950
£5,950 × 0.091			541
6.4.85 pool	850	5,950	6,491
Indexed rise: April 1985 to September 1995			
£6,491 × 0.589			3,823
17.9.95 acquisition	1,150	5,200	5,200
	2,000	11,150	15,514
Indexed rise: September 1995 to April 1998			
£15,514 × 0.080			1,241
			16,755
19.12.06 disposal	(2,000)	(11,150)	(16,755)
Balance of pool	—	—	—

	£
Sale proceeds (2,000 × £10.50)	21,000
Cost (as above)	11,150
Unindexed gain	9,850
Indexation allowance (£16,755 − £11,150)	5,605
Chargeable gain (subject to TAPER RELIEF (228))	£4,245

1982 holding		£	£
Sale proceeds (1,200 + 1,400) × £10.50		27,300	27,300
Cost (£3,000 + £5,000)		8,000	
Market value 31.3.82 (2,600 × £4)			10,400
Unindexed gain		19,300	16,900
Indexation allowance £10,400 × 1.047		10,889	10,889
Gain after indexation		£8,411	£6,011
Chargeable gain (subject to TAPER RELIEF (228))			£6,011

10.11.62 acquisition	£	£	£
Sale proceeds (750 × £10.50)	7,875	7,875	7,875
Cost	600		
Market value 6.4.65 (750 × £1.60)		1,200	
Market value 31.3.82 (750 × £4)			3,000
Unindexed gain	7,275	6,675	4,875
Indexation allowance £3,000 × 1.047	3,141	3,141	3,141
Gain after indexation	£4,134	£3,534	£1,734
Chargeable gain (subject to TAPER RELIEF (228))			£1,734

9.1.57 acquisition (part)	£	£	£
Sale proceeds (650 × £10.50)	6,825	6,825	6,825
Cost (650 × £0.70)	455		
Market value 6.4.65 (650 × £1.60)		1,040	
Market value 31.3.82 (650 × £4)			2,600
Unindexed gain	6,370	5,785	4,225
Indexation allowance £2,600 × 1.047	2,722	2,722	2,722
Gain after indexation	£3,648	£3,063	£1,503
Chargeable gain (subject to TAPER RELIEF (228))			£1,503

Summary of chargeable gains	Number of shares	Chargeable gain £
Section 104 holding	2,000	4,245
1982 holding	2,600	6,011
10.11.62 acquisition	750	1,734
9.1.57 acquisition (part)	650	1,503
	6,000	£13,493

Remaining shares
850 acquired on 9.1.57 for £595

204.1   Assets held on 6 April 1965

(ii) Election made to substitute 1965 market value

Identify 6,000 shares on a LIFO basis as follows

Section 104 holding
Disposal of 2,000 shares as in (i) above   £4,245

1982 holding	Shares		Pool cost
			£
9.1.57	1,500 × £1.60		2,400
10.11.62	750 × £1.60		1,200
15.7.69	1,200		3,000
12.10.80	1,400		5,000
	4,850		11,600
19.12.06 disposal	4,000	4,000/4,850 × £11,600	9,567
Remaining shares	850		£2,033

	£	£
Sale proceeds (4,000 × £10.50)	42,000	42,000
Cost (as above)	9,567	
Market value 31.3.82 (4,000 × £4)		16,000
Unindexed gain	32,433	26,000
Indexation allowance £16,000 × 1.047	16,752	16,752
Gain after indexation	£15,681	£9,248

Chargeable gain (subject to TAPER RELIEF (228))   £9,248

Summary of chargeable gains/allowable losses	Number of shares	Chargeable gain/(loss)
		£
Section 104 holding	2,000	4,245
1982 holding	4,000	9,248
	6,000	£13,493

Notes

(*a*) Because re-basing to 31 March 1982 applies in this case, the result is the same whether or not the election to substitute 6 April 1965 value has been made, but with a lower 31 March 1982 value the computations could produce differing overall gains/losses.

(*b*) Note that indexation is based on 31 March 1982 value whenever this gives the greater allowance, and that comparisons are made between gains *after* indexation and *before* taper relief.

(*c*) Other than for the purposes of corporation tax on chargeable gains, indexation allowance is frozen at its April 1998 level. Therefore, the indexation factor for April 1998 is used in respect of disposals in a later month (and expenditure incurred in April 1998 or later does not attract indexation allowance at all). See 212 INDEXATION.

(*d*) See 227.1 SHARES AND SECURITIES—IDENTIFICATION RULES for rules for matching disposals after 5 April 1998 with acquisitions after that date (not illustrated in this example).

204.2 **LAND REFLECTING DEVELOPMENT VALUE** [*TCGA 1992, Sch 2 paras 9–15*]

K sells a building plot, on which planning permission has just been obtained, in November 2006 for £200,000. He acquired the plot by gift from his father in 1958 when its value was £2,000. The market value was £5,000 at 6 April 1965 and £10,000 at 31 March 1982, and the current use value in November 2006 is £15,000. The indexation factor for March 1982 to April 1998 is 1.047.

	£	£	£
Sale proceeds	200,000	200,000	200,000
Cost	2,000		
Market value 6.4.65		5,000	
Market value 31.3.82			10,000
Unindexed gain	198,000	195,000	190,000
Indexation allowance			
£10,000 × 1.047	10,470	10,470	10,470
Gain after indexation	£187,530	£184,530	£179,530
Chargeable gain (subject to TAPER RELIEF (228))			£179,530

Notes

(*a*) Time apportionment would have substantially reduced the gain of £187,530, using cost, such that re-basing to 31 March 1982 would have given a greater gain than that based on cost and would not therefore have applied. However, as the plot has been sold for a price in excess of its current use value, no time apportionment can be claimed.

(*b*) Gains must be compared after applying the indexation allowance, which is based on 31 March 1982 value, this being greater than either cost or 6 April 1965 value.

(*c*) In this case, the gain is computed in accordance with the rules in 205 ASSETS HELD ON 31 MARCH 1982 as the gain by reference to 31 March 1982 value is lower than the gain by reference to 6 April 1965 value which in turn is lower than the gain by reference to cost.

204.3 Assets held on 6 April 1965

204.3 **OTHER ASSETS** [*TCGA 1992, Sch 2 paras 16–19; FA 1996, Sch 21 para 42(1)(3)*]

(A) Chattels

M inherited a painting on the death of his mother in 1940, when it was valued for probate at £5,000. On 5 October 2006 he sold the painting for £270,000 net. The painting's value was £130,000 at 6 April 1965, but only £125,000 at 31 March 1982. The indexation factor for March 1982 to April 1998 is 1.047.

(i) Time apportionment

Period of ownership since 6 April 1945	(note (*a*))	61 years 6 months
Period of ownership since 6 April 1965		41 years 6 months

	£
	£
Unindexed gain (£270,000 – £5,000)	265,000
Indexation allowance £125,000 × 1.047 (note (*b*))	130,875
	£134,125

Gain after indexation £134,125 × $\dfrac{41\text{y } 6\text{m}}{61\text{y } 6\text{m}}$ (note (*c*))	£90,507

(ii) Election for 6.4.65 value

	£
Sale proceeds	270,000
Market value 6.4.65	130,000
Unindexed gain	140,000
Indexation allowance £130,000 × 1.047 (note (*b*))	136,110
Gain after indexation	£3,890

Election for 6.4.65 value is beneficial, subject to re-basing.

(iii) Re-basing to 1982

	£
Sale proceeds	270,000
Market value 31.3.82	125,000
Unindexed gain	145,000
Indexation allowance £130,000 × 1.047 (note (*b*))	136,110
Gain after indexation	£8,890

Re-basing cannot increase a gain. [*TCGA 1992, s 35(3)(a)*]. **Therefore, the gain of £3,890 stands** (subject to TAPER RELIEF (228), and see note (*d*)) **and the election for 6.4.65 value is beneficial.**

Notes

(*a*) Under time apportionment, the period of ownership is limited to that after 5 April 1945.

(*b*) In (i) above, indexation is based on 31.3.82 value, being greater than cost — it cannot be based on 6 April 1965 value as this does not enter into the calculation. In (ii), indexation is on the higher of 31.3.82 value and 6.4.65 value. This is also the case in (iii) as one is comparing the position using 6.4.65 value and 31.3.82 value. See *TCGA 1992, s 55(1)(2)*.

(*c*)   The time apportionment calculation is applied to the gain *after* indexation (*Smith v Schofield HL 1993, 65 TC 669, [1993] STC 268*).

(*d*)   Taper relief should be computed by reference to the *chargeable* gain. Therefore, if time apportionment had produced the lower gain (disregarding taper relief at this stage), it is the time-apportioned gain that would be tapered. This is because taper relief comes after all other reliefs apart from the annual exemption. [*TCGA 1992, s 2A(1)(2)*].

(B) Land and buildings

X acquired land on 5 June 1960 as a distribution in specie on liquidation of his company. The value of the land was then £7,250. He acquired access land adjoining the property for £2,750 on 1 January 1961 and, having obtained planning consent, on 30 July 1963 incurred expenditure of £15,000 in building houses on the land, which were let. On 6 September 2006, X sells the houses with vacant possession for £300,000, net of expenses. The value of the houses and land is £20,000 at 6 April 1965 and £100,000 at 31 March 1982. The indexation factor for March 1982 to April 1998 is 1.047.

The gain using time apportionment is

	£	£
Net proceeds of sale		300,000
Deduct Cost of land	7,250	
Cost of addition	2,750	
Cost of building	15,000	25,000
Unindexed gain		275,000
Indexation allowance £100,000 × 1.047		104,700
Gain after indexation		£170,300

Apportion to allowable expenditure   (note (*c*))

	£	£
(i) Land $\dfrac{7,250}{25,000} \times £170,300$	49,387	
Time apportion £49,387 $\times \dfrac{41\text{y }5\text{m}}{46\text{y }3\text{m}}$		44,225
(ii) Addition $\dfrac{2,750}{25,000} \times £170,300$	18,733	
Time apportion £18,733 $\times \dfrac{41\text{y }5\text{m}}{45\text{y }8\text{m}}$		16,990
		c/f £61,215

204.3   Assets held on 6 April 1965

	£	£
		b/f 61,215
(iii) Building $\dfrac{15,000}{25,000} \times £170,300$	102,180	
Time apportion $£102,180 \times \dfrac{41\text{y } 5\text{m}}{43\text{y } 1\text{m}}$		98,227
Gain after indexation and time apportionment		£159,442

The gain using re-basing to 1982 is

	£
Net proceeds of sale	300,000
Market value at 31.3.82	100,000
Unindexed gain	200,000
Indexation allowance	
$£100,000 \times 1.047$	104,700
Gain	£95,300

Chargeable gain (subject to
TAPER RELIEF (228), and see note (*d*))   £95,300

Notes

(*a*)   An election for 6 April 1965 valuation could not be favourable, even were it not for the effect of re-basing, as the value is less than historic costs.

(*b*)   It is the gain/loss *after* time apportionment that is compared with the gain/loss produced by re-basing. [*TCGA 1992, Sch 3 para 6*].

(*c*)   The time apportionment calculation is applied to the gain *after* indexation (*Smith v Schofield HL 1993, 65 TC 669, [1993] STC 268*).

(*d*)   Taper relief should be computed by reference to the *chargeable* gain. Therefore, if time apportionment had produced the lower gain (disregarding taper relief at this stage), it is the time-apportioned gain that would be tapered. This is because taper relief comes after all other reliefs apart from the annual exemption. [*TCGA 1992, s 2A(1)(2); FA 1998, s 121(1)(4)*].

(C) Unquoted shares

On 6 April 1953, A acquired 5,000 shares in C Ltd, an unquoted company, for £15,201. At 6 April 1965, the value of the holding was £15,000. A sells the shares (his entire holding in the company) on 6 April 2006 for £75,000. The indexation factor for the period March 1982 to April 1998 is 1.047 (note (*b*)). No election for universal 31 March 1982 re-basing is made but the market value of the holding at that date is agreed at £17,000.

The gain using time apportionment is as follows

Total period of ownership: 53 years

Period after 6 April 1965:   41 years

	£
Proceeds	75,000
Cost	15,201
Unindexed gain	59,799
Indexation allowance:	
31.3.82 value £17,000 × 1.047	17,799
Gain after indexation	£42,000
Gain after time apportionment: £42,000 × 41/53	£32,490

The gain with an election to use 6.4.65 value is as follows

	£
Proceeds	75,000
6.4.65 value	15,000
Unindexed gain	60,000
Indexation allowance:	
31.3.82 value £17,000 × 1.047	17,799
Gain after indexation	£42,201

The gain with re-basing to 1982 is as follows

	£
Proceeds	75,000
31.3.82 value	17,000
Unindexed gain	58,000
Indexation allowance:	
31.3.82 value £17,000 × 1.047	17,799
Gain after indexation	£40,201

Time apportionment is more beneficial than an election for 6 April 1965 value. Re-basing does not apply as it cannot increase a gain. The chargeable gain is therefore £32,307 (subject to TAPER RELIEF (228), and see note (*a*)).

Note

(*a*)   Taper relief should be computed by reference to the *chargeable* gain. Therefore, if, as in this example, time apportionment produces the lower gain (disregarding taper relief in making the comparison), it is the time-apportioned gain that is tapered. This is because taper relief comes after all other reliefs apart from the annual exemption. [*TCGA 1992, s 2A(1)(2); FA 1998, s 121(1)(4)*]. See generally 228 TAPER RELIEF.

204.3   Assets held on 6 April 1965

(D) Unquoted shares — share exchange before 6 April 1965 [*TCGA 1992, Sch 2 para 19(1)(3)*]

N purchased 5,000 £1 ordinary shares in R Ltd, an unquoted company, on 1 January 1961. The purchase price was £3 per share, a total of £15,000. On 1 December 1964, R Ltd was acquired by D Ltd, an unquoted company, as a result of which N received 10,000 8% convertible preference shares in D Ltd in exchange for his holding of R shares. In November 2006, N sold the D Ltd shares for £4.45 per share. The market value of the D Ltd shares was £2.03 per share at 6 April 1965 but only £1.50 per share at 31 March 1982. The indexation factor for March 1982 to April 1998 is 1.047.

The gain, disregarding re-basing, is

	£
Disposal consideration 10,000 at £4.45	44,500
Allowable cost 10,000 at £2.03	20,300
Unindexed gain	24,200
Indexation allowance £20,300 × 1.047	21,254
Gain after indexation	£2,946

The gain using re-basing to 1982 is

	£
Disposal consideration (as above)	44,500
Market value 31.3.82 10,000 at £1.50	15,000
Unindexed gain	29,500
Indexation allowance £20,300 × 1.047	21,254
Gain after indexation	£8,246

The overall result is

	£
Chargeable gain (subject to TAPER RELIEF (228))	£2,946

Notes

(a)   Subject to re-basing, allowable cost *must* be taken as 6.4.65 value.

(b)   Indexation is based on the greater of 31.3.82 value and 6.4.65 value. [*TCGA 1992, s 55(1)(2)*].

(c)   Where the effect of re-basing would be to increase a gain, re-basing does not apply. [*TCGA 1992, s 35(3)(a)*].

(d)   By concession (ESC D10), CGT is not charged on a disposal of the *entire* new shareholding on more than the actual gain realised, i.e. by reference to original cost but without time apportionment.

(E) Unquoted shares — share exchange after 5 April 1965 [*TCGA 1992, Sch 2 para 19(2)(3)*]

S acquired 10,000 £1 ordinary shares in L Ltd at their probate value of £5,000 on 31 May 1959. The shares are not quoted, and their value at 6 April 1965 was £6,000. On 1 September 1989, the shares were acquired by R plc, in exchange for its own ordinary shares on the basis of 1 for 2. The offer valued L ordinary shares at £2.23 per share. In February 2007, S sells his 5,000 R shares for £8.60 per share. The agreed value of the L Ltd shares at 31 March 1982 was £2.05 per share.

Indexation factors	March 1982 to September 1989	0.468
	September 1989 to April 1998	0.395
	March 1982 to April 1998	1.047

The gain without re-basing to 1982 is computed as follows

(i) Using time apportionment

Deemed disposal at 1.9.89:

	£
Proceeds (market value £2.23 × 10,000)	22,300
Cost	5,000
Unindexed gain	17,300
Indexation allowance	
MV 31.3.82 10,000 × £2.05 × 0.468	9,594
Gain after indexation	£7,706

Gain after time apportionment:

$$£7,706 \times \frac{24y\ 5m}{30y\ 3m}$$ £6,220

Actual disposal in February 2007:

	£
Proceeds 5,000 × £8.60	43,000
Deemed acquisition cost at 1.9.89	22,300
Unindexed gain	20,700
Indexation allowance £22,300 × 0.395	8,809
Gain after indexation	£11,891

Total gain 2006/07 £(6,220 + 11,891)	£18,111

(ii) With election for 6.4.65 value

	£
Disposal consideration	43,000
Allowable cost	6,000
Unindexed gain	37,000
Indexation allowance 10,000 × £2.05 × 1.047	21,463
Gain	£15,537

Subject to re-basing, the election is beneficial.

204.3   Assets held on 6 April 1965

The gain using re-basing to 1982 is

	£
Disposal consideration	43,000
Market value 31.3.82 10,000 × £2.05	20,500
Unindexed gain	22,500
Indexation allowance £20,500 × 1.047	21,463
Gain after indexation	£1,037

The overall result is

Chargeable gain (subject to TAPER RELIEF (228))	£1,037

Re-basing applies as it produces a smaller gain than that using 6 April 1965 value.

Notes

(a)   The deemed disposal on 1 September 1989 is *only* for the purposes of *TCGA 1992, Sch 2 para 16* (time apportionment).

(b)   If an election is made for 6 April 1965 value, no valuation is required at 1 September 1989.

(F) Part disposals after 5 April 1965 [*TCGA 1992, s 42, Sch 2 para 16(8)*]
H bought land for £15,000 on 31 October 1960. Its value at 6 April 1965 was £17,200. On 1 February 1988, H sold part of the land for £50,000, the balance being then worth £200,000. On 9 April 2006, H gives the remaining land to his daughter. Its value is then £300,000. The agreed value of the total estate at 31 March 1982 was £150,000 and H made a claim on the February 1988 disposal for that value to be used for indexation purposes under the law then in force.

Indexation factors	March 1982 to February 1988	0.305
	March 1982 to April 1998	1.047

1988 disposal

	£
Proceeds of part disposal	50,000
Deduct allowable cost $\dfrac{50,000}{50,000 + 200,000} \times £15,000$	3,000
Unindexed gain	47,000
Indexation allowance £150,000 $\times \dfrac{50,000}{50,000 + 200,000} = £30,000$	
£30,000 × 0.305	9,150
Gain after indexation	£37,850

Time apportionment

Chargeable gain $\dfrac{22y\ 10m}{27y\ 3m} \times £37,850$	£31,715

If an election were made to substitute 6 April 1965 valuation, the computation would be

	£
Proceeds of part disposal	50,000
Deduct allowable cost $\dfrac{50,000}{50,000 + 200,000} \times £17,200$	3,440
Unindexed gain	46,560
Indexation allowance £150,000 $\times \dfrac{50,000}{50,000 + 200,000} = £30,000$	
£30,000 × 0.305	9,150
Chargeable gain	£37,410

An election would not be beneficial.

204.3 Assets held on 6 April 1965

2006 disposal

The gain without re-basing to 1982 is as follows

Computation of entire gain over period of ownership:

	£
Proceeds	300,000
Cost £(15,000 − 3,000)	12,000
Unindexed gain	288,000
Indexation allowance	
MV 31.3.82 £(150,000 − 30,000) × 1.047	125,640
Gain after indexation	£162,360(A)

Computation of gain for period 31.10.60 − 1.2.88:

	£
Market value at date of part disposal	200,000
Cost £(15,000 − 3,000)	12,000
Unindexed gain	188,000
Indexation allowance £(150,000 − 30,000) × 0.305	36,600
Gain after indexation	£151,400(B)

$$\text{Time apportionment } £151,400 \times \frac{22\text{y }10\text{m}}{27\text{y }3\text{m}} \qquad £126,861(C)$$

Balance of gain (1.2.88 to 9.4.06) ((A) − (B)) £10,960(D)

Chargeable gain (subject to re-basing) ((C) + (D)) £137,821

The gain using re-basing to 1982 is as follows

	£
Disposal proceeds	300,000
Market value 31.3.82 £150,000 × $\frac{12,000}{15,000}$ (note (b))	120,000
Unindexed gain	180,000
Indexation allowance £120,000 × 1.047	125,640
Gain after indexation	£54,360

The overall result is

Chargeable gain (subject to TAPER RELIEF (228)) £54,360

Re-basing applies as it produces neither a larger gain nor a loss.

Notes

(*a*)   The deemed disposal on 1 February 1988 is only for the purposes of *TCGA 1992, Sch 2 para 16(3)–(5)* (time apportionment). For re-basing purposes, the asset is still regarded as having been held at 31 March 1982.

(*b*)   Where there has been a part disposal after 31 March 1982 and before 6 April 1988 of an asset held at 31 March 1982, the proportion of 31 March 1982 value to be brought into account in the re-basing calculation is that which the cost previously unallowed bears to the total cost, giving the same effect as if re-basing had applied to the part disposal. [*TCGA 1992, Sch 3 para 4(1)*].

(*c*)   HMRC will also accept an alternative basis of calculation on the part disposal of land. Under this method, the part disposed of is treated as a separate asset and any fair and reasonable method of apportioning part of the total cost to it will be accepted e.g. a reasonable valuation of that part at the acquisition date. (HMRC Statement of Practice SP D1.)

(*d*)   The time apportionment calculation is applied to the gain *after* indexation (*Smith v Schofield HL 1993, 65 TC 669, [1993] STC 268*).

205   Assets held on 31 March 1982

205.1 GENERAL COMPUTATION OF GAINS/LOSSES [*TCGA 1992, s 35, Sch 3*]

(A)

Rodney purchased a painting on 1 October 1979 for £50,000 (including costs of acquisition) and sold it at auction for £160,000 (net of selling expenses) on 15 August 2006 (his only disposal in 2006/07). Its value at 31 March 1982 was £70,000 and the indexation factor for the period March 1982 to April 1998 is 1.047 (see note (*f*)).

	£	£
Net sale proceeds	160,000	160,000
Cost	50,000	
Market value 31.3.82		70,000
Unindexed gain	110,000	90,000
Indexation allowance £70,000 × 1.047	73,290	73,290
Gain after indexation	£36,710	£16,710

	£
Chargeable gain (subject to taper relief)	16,710
Deduct Taper Relief	
(£16,710 @ 35% — non-business asset held 8 + 1 years)	5,849
Chargeable gain	£10,861

Notes

(*a*)   The asset is deemed to have been sold and immediately re-acquired at its market value at 31 March 1982. [*TCGA 1992, s 35(1)(2)*].

(*b*)   Re-basing does not apply if it would produce a larger gain or larger loss than would otherwise be the case, nor if it would turn a gain into a loss or vice versa, nor if the disposal would otherwise be a no gain/no loss disposal. [*TCGA 1992, s 35(3)(4)*].

(*c*)   An *irrevocable* election may be made to treat, broadly speaking, *all* assets held on 31 March 1982 as having been sold and re-acquired at their market value on that date, in which case the restrictions in (*b*) above will not apply. [*TCGA 1992, s 35(5)*]. If the election had been made in this example, the gain would still be £16,710, but there would have been no need to compute the gain by reference to cost and make a comparison with that using re-basing.

There are some minor exclusions from the rule that the election must extend to all assets. [*TCGA 1992, Sch 3 para 7*]. There are also special rules for groups of companies. [*TCGA 1992, Sch 3 paras 8, 9*].

(*d*)   Indexation is automatically based on 31 March 1982 value, without the need to claim such treatment, unless a greater allowance would be produced by reference to cost. [*TCGA 1992, s 55(1)(2)*]. See also 212.1(C) INDEXATION.

(*e*)   See also 204 ASSETS HELD ON 6 APRIL 1965 for the general application of the re-basing provisions to such assets. See 212.2(A)(C) INDEXATION for the position as regards an asset acquired by means of a no gain/no loss transfer from a person who held it at 31 March 1982.

(*f*)   Other than for the purposes of corporation tax on chargeable gains, indexation allowance is frozen at its April 1998 level. Therefore, the indexation factor for April 1998 is used in respect of disposals in a later month. See 212 INDEXATION.

(B)

The facts are as in (A) above, except that net sale proceeds amount to £60,000.

	£	£
Net sale proceeds	60,000	60,000
Cost	50,000	
Market value 31.3.82		70,000
Unindexed gain/(loss)	10,000	(10,000)
Indexation allowance (as in (A))		
but restricted to	10,000	—
Gain/(loss)	Nil	£(10,000)
Chargeable gain/(allowable loss)	Nil	

Notes

(a) Re-basing does not apply as it cannot disturb a no gain/no loss position. [*TCGA 1992, s 35(3)(c)*].

(b) An election under *TCGA 1992, s 35(5)* would produce an allowable loss of £10,000 (but must extend to all assets).

(C)

The facts are as in (A) above, except that net sale proceeds amount to £135,000.

	£	£
Net sale proceeds	135,000	135,000
Cost	50,000	
Market value 31.3.82		70,000
Unindexed gain	85,000	65,000
Indexation allowance (as in (A))	73,290	
Indexation allowance (as in (A))		
but restricted to		65,000
Gain	£11,710	Nil
Chargeable gain/(allowable loss)		Nil

Note

(a) Re-basing applies as it produces a no gain/no loss position compared to a gain otherwise.

205.1   Assets held on 31 March 1982

(D)

Albert acquired a holding of D plc quoted shares for £11,000 net in January 1980. At 31 March 1982, their value had fallen to £8,000. On 29 April 2006, Albert sold the entire holding for £25,000 net (his only disposal in 2006/07). The indexation factor for the period March 1982 to April 1998 is 1.047.

	£	£
Proceeds	25,000	25,000
Cost	11,000	
Market value 31.3.82		8,000
Unindexed gain	14,000	17,000
Indexation allowance £11,000 × 1.047	11,517	11,517
Gain after indexation	£2,483	£5,483

	£
Chargeable gain (subject to taper relief)	2,483
Deduct Taper Relief	
(£2,483 @ 35% — non-business asset held 8 + 1 years)	869
Chargeable gain	£1,614

Notes

(*a*)   Re-basing does not apply as its effect would be to increase a gain.

(*b*)   Indexation is based on cost as that is greater than 31 March 1982 value.

(*c*)   If a universal re-basing election had been made (under *TCGA 1992, s 35(5)*), the chargeable gain (before taper relief) would have been £5,483.

(E)

Cassandra acquired a holding of E Ltd shares for £14,000 net in January 1980. At 31 March 1982, their value stood at £17,000. Cassandra sold the shares in April 2006 for £10,000 net.

	£	£
Proceeds	10,000	10,000
Cost	14,000	
Market value 31.3.82		17,000
Unindexed loss (no indexation due)	£4,000	£7,000
Allowable loss	£4,000	

Notes

(*a*)   Re-basing does not apply as its effect would be to increase a loss.

(*b*)   Indexation is not available in either calculation as it cannot increase a loss.

(*c*)   If a universal re-basing election had been made (under *TCGA 1992, s 35(5)*), the allowable loss would have been £7,000, but the election must extend to all assets.

205.2 **DEFERRED CHARGES ON GAINS BEFORE 31 MARCH 1982** [*TCGA 1992, s 36, Sch 4*]

Kirk purchased 3,000 unquoted ordinary shares in W Limited for £18,000 on 1 January 1980 and later gave them to his son, Michael, claiming gifts hold-over relief under legislation then in force. Michael sells the shares for £50,000 (net) on 10 June 2006. The shares had a value of £22,000 at 31 March 1982.

Assuming the gift to have taken place on

  (i)   1 February 1982 (market value of shares £21,000),
  (ii)   30 April 1994 (market value £42,000), and
  (iii) 1 June 1985 (market value £30,000),

the capital gains position is as set out below. The relevant indexation factors are

March 1982 to June 1985	0.202
March 1982 to April 1994	0.815
March 1982 to April 1998	1.047
June 1985 to April 1998	0.704
April 1994 to April 1998	0.128

(i) Gift on 1 February 1982

Kirk's chargeable gain (deferred) (£21,000 − £18,000)	£3,000

Michael's acquisition cost (£21,000 − £3,000)	£18,000

Michael's chargeable gain is

	£	£
Proceeds 10.6.06	50,000	50,000
Cost (as above)	18,000	
Market value 31.3.82		22,000
Unindexed gain	32,000	28,000
Indexation allowance £22,000 × 1.047	23,034	23,034
Gain after indexation	£8,966	£4,966
Chargeable gain 2006/07 (note (*e*))		£4,966

The deferred gain of £3,000 effectively falls out of charge as Michael held the shares at 31.3.82 and thus receives the benefit of re-basing to 1982.

(ii) Gift on 30 April 1994

Kirk's chargeable gain is

	£	£
Disposal value	42,000	42,000
Cost	18,000	
Market value 31.3.82		22,000
Unindexed gain	24,000	20,000
Indexation allowance £22,000 × 0.815	17,930	17,930
Gain after indexation	£6,070	£2,070
Chargeable gain (deferred)		£2,070

205.2 Assets held on 31 March 1982

Michael's chargeable gain is

	£	£
Proceeds 10.6.06		50,000
Cost	42,000	
Deduct deferred gain	2,070	
	39,930	
Indexation allowance £39,930 × 0.128	5,111	45,041
Chargeable gain 2006/07 (note (*e*))		£4,959

Michael cannot re-base to 1982 as he did not hold the shares at 31.3.82. However, as the deferred gain was itself computed by reference to the 31.3.82 value, he has effectively received full relief for the uplift in value between 1.1.80 and 31.3.82. The small difference between his gain of £4,959 and that of £4,966 in (i) above is due to the rounding of indexation factors to three decimal places.

(iii) Gift on 1 June 1985

Kirk's chargeable gain is

	£	£
Disposal value		30,000
Cost	18,000	
Indexation allowance £22,000 × 0.202	4,444	22,444
Chargeable gain (deferred)		£7,556

It is assumed that a claim would have been made to base indexation on the 31.3.82 value, this being greater than cost.

Michael's chargeable gain is

	£	£
Proceeds 10.6.06		50,000
Cost	30,000	
Deduct one-half of deferred gain		
£7,556 × $\frac{1}{2}$	3,778	
	26,222	
Indexation allowance £26,222 × 0.704	18,460	44,682
Chargeable gain 2006/07 (note (*e*))		£5,318

Michael cannot benefit from re-basing to 1982 as he did not hold the shares at 31.3.82, nor is the deferred gain itself calculated by reference to the re-basing rules as the disposal (i.e. the gift) took place before 6.4.88. Under *TCGA 1992, s 36, Sch 4 para 1(a), para 2*, the deduction in respect of a deferred gain is halved where the deferral took place after 31.3.82 and before 6.4.88 and was, wholly or partly, in respect of a chargeable gain accruing on an asset held at 31.3.82, thus giving some relief, albeit on an arbitrary basis.

Notes

(*a*) A claim for the deduction to be halved must be made by the first anniversary of 31 January following the year of assessment in which the ultimate disposal takes place. [*TCGA 1992, Sch 4 para 9; FA 1996, Sch 21 para 43*].

(*b*) These provisions apply not only to gifts hold-over relief but to a number of situations in which gains are held over or rolled over, as listed in *TCGA 1992, Sch 4 para 2(5)*, of which the other most common example is rollover relief on replacement of business assets under *TCGA 1992, s 152*. [*TCGA 1992, Sch 4 para 1(a), para 2*].

(*c*)   There are special rules where the disposal giving rise to the deferral is preceded by a no gain/no loss disposal (as defined by *TCGA 1992, s 35(3)(d)*) and where the ultimate disposal is preceded by a no gain/no loss disposal. [*TCGA 1992, Sch 4 paras 5–7*].

(*d*)   See 211 HOLD-OVER RELIEFS and 224 ROLLOVER RELIEF—REPLACEMENT OF BUSINESS ASSETS for the general application of these reliefs.

(*e*)   In all cases, the 2006/07 chargeable gain is subject to TAPER RELIEF (228), which is given by reference to the *donee's* post-5 April 1998 period of ownership.

206   Capital Sums Derived from Assets

206.1 GENERAL [*TCGA 1992, s 22(1)*]

A Ltd holds the remainder of a 99-year lease of land, under which it has mineral rights. The lease, which commenced in 1989, was acquired in April 1998 by assignment for £80,000. Following a proposal to extract minerals, the freeholder pays A Ltd £100,000 in June 2006 in consideration of relinquishing the mineral rights, in order to prevent such development. The value of the lease after the alteration is £150,000.

	£
Disposal proceeds	100,000
Allowable cost $\dfrac{100,000}{100,000 + 150,000} \times £80,000$	32,000
Gain subject to indexation from April 1998 to June 2006	£68,000

206.2 DEFERRED CONSIDERATION

Z owns 2,000 £1 ordinary shares in B Ltd, for which he subscribed at par in August 1998. On 31 March 2002, he and the other shareholders in B Ltd sold their shares to another company for £10 per share plus a further unquantified cash amount calculated by means of a formula relating to the future profits of B Ltd. The value in March 2002 of the deferred consideration was estimated at £2 per share. On 30 April 2006, Z receives a further £4.20 per share under the sale agreement.

2001/02

	£	£
Disposal proceeds 2,000 at £10	20,000	
Value of rights 2,000 at £2	4,000	24,000
Cost of acquisition		2,000
Chargeable gain (subject to TAPER RELIEF (228))		£22,000

2006/07

	£
Disposal of rights to deferred consideration	
Proceeds 2,000 × £4.20	8,400
Deemed cost of acquiring rights	4,000
Chargeable gain (subject to TAPER RELIEF (228))	£4,400

Notes

(*a*)   A right to unquantified and contingent future consideration on the disposal of an asset is itself an asset, and the future consideration when received is a capital sum derived from that asset (*Marren v Ingles HL 1980, 54 TC 76* and *Marson v Marriage Ch D 1979, 54 TC 59*).

(*b*)   See 226.4 SHARES AND SECURITIES for position where deferred consideration is to be satisfied in shares and/or debentures in the acquiring company.

(*c*)   See also 216.4 LOSSES for the election to treat a loss arising after 9 April 2003 on disposal of a right to deferred unascertainable consideration as accruing in an earlier year.

206.3 **RECEIPT OF COMPENSATION** [*TCGA 1992, ss 22, 23*]

(A)

C owns a freehold warehouse which is badly damaged by fire as a result of inflammable goods having been inadequately packaged. The value of the warehouse after the fire is £90,000, and it cost £120,000 in 1994. The owner of the goods is held liable for the damage and pays C £60,000 compensation in October 2006.

	£
Disposal proceeds	60,000
Allowable cost $\dfrac{60,000}{60,000 + 90,000} \times £120,000$	48,000
Chargeable gain 2006/07 subject to indexation to April 1998 and taper relief	£12,000

(B) Restoration using insurance moneys

A diamond necklace owned by D cost £100,000 in 1996. D is involved in a motor accident in which the necklace is damaged. Its value is reduced to £80,000. D receives £40,000 under an insurance policy in May 2006 and spends £45,000 on having the necklace restored.

(i) No claim under *TCGA 1992, s 23*

	£
Disposal proceeds	40,000
Allowable cost $\dfrac{40,000}{40,000 + 80,000} \times £100,000$	33,333
Chargeable gain 2006/07 subject to indexation to April 1998 and taper relief	£6,667
Allowable cost in relation to subsequent disposal £100,000 − £33,333 + £45,000	£111,667

(ii) Claim under *TCGA 1992, s 23*

No chargeable gain arises in 2006/07

Allowable cost originally	100,000
Deduct Amount received on claim	40,000
	60,000
Add Expenditure on restoration	45,000
Allowable cost in relation to subsequent disposal	£105,000

206.3   Capital Sums Derived from Assets

(C) Part application of capital sum received

E Ltd is the owner of a large estate consisting mainly of parkland which it acquired for
£150,000 in August 1992. It grants a one-year licence in August 2006 to an exploration
company to prospect for minerals, in consideration for a capital sum of £50,000. The
exploration proves unsuccessful and on expiry of the licence E Ltd spends £20,000 on
restoration of the drilling sites to their former state. The market value of the estate after
granting the licence is £350,000, and it is £400,000 after restoration.

(i) No claim under *TCGA 1992, s 23(3)*

	£
Disposal proceeds	50,000
Deduct Allowable cost $\dfrac{50,000}{50,000 + 350,000} \times £150,000$	18,750
Gain subject to indexation from August 1992 to August 2006	£31,250
Allowable expenditure remaining £150,000 − £18,750 + £20,000	£151,250

(ii) Claim made under *TCGA 1992, s 23(3)*

	£
Deemed disposal proceeds (£50,000 − £20,000)	30,000
Deduct	
Allowable cost $\dfrac{30,000}{30,000 + 400,000} \times £(150,000 + 20,000)$	11,860
Gain subject to indexation to August 2006	£18,140
Allowable expenditure remaining £150,000 − £20,000 − £11,860 + £20,000	£138,140

(D) Capital sum exceeding allowable expenditure

F inherited a painting in 1980 when it was valued at £2,000. Its value at 31 March 1982
was £3,000. In March 1987, by which time its value had increased considerably, the
painting suffered damage whilst on loan to an art gallery and F received £10,000
compensation. The value of the painting was then £30,000. It then cost F £9,800 to have
the painting restored. In June 2006, he sells the painting for £50,000.

(i) No election under *TCGA 1992, s 23(2)*

	£
Disposal proceeds March 1987	10,000
Allowable cost $\dfrac{10,000}{10,000 + 30,000} \times £2,000$	500
Gain subject to indexation 1986/87	£9,500
Allowable cost in relation to subsequent disposal £2,000 − £500 + £9,800	£11,300

	£	£
Disposal proceeds June 2006	50,000	50,000
Allowable cost without re-basing	11,300	
Allowable cost with re-basing		

$$£3,000 \times \frac{30,000}{10,000 + 30,000} = £2,250 + £9,800 \qquad 12,050$$

	£	£
Gain subject to indexation 2006/07	£38,700	£37,950

It is clear that re-basing will apply and the pre-tapered gain will be £37,950 less indexation allowance to April 1998, based on £12,050.

(ii) Election under _TCGA 1992, s 23(2)_

	£
Disposal proceeds March 1987	10,000
Less allowable expenditure	2,000
Gain subject to indexation 1986/87	£8,000
Allowable cost in relation to subsequent disposal £2,000 − £2,000 + £9,800	£9,800

	£	£
Disposal proceeds June 2006	50,000	50,000
Allowable cost without re-basing	9,800	
Allowable cost with re-basing (note (_b_)) £3,000 − £2,000 + £9,800		10,800
Gain subject to indexation 2006/07	£40,200	£39,200

Again, re-basing will clearly apply and the pre-tapered gain will be £39,200 less indexation allowance to April 1998, based on £10,800.

Notes

(_a_)   Although not illustrated in this example, indexation allowance must be deducted before comparing the positions with and without re-basing in order to ascertain whether or not re-basing applies.

(_b_)   Where there is a disposal after 5 April 1989 to which re-basing applies and, if re-basing had not applied, the allowable expenditure would have fallen to be reduced under _TCGA 1992, s 23(2)_ by reference to a capital sum received after 31 March 1982 but before 6 April 1988, the 31 March 1982 value is reduced by the amount previously allowed against the capital sum. [_TCGA 1992, Sch 3 para 4(2)_].

206.3 Capital Sums Derived from Assets

(E) Indexation allowance and taper relief [*TCGA 1992, s 2A, s 53(1)(1A)(3), s 57; FA 2002, s 46*]

A owns a freehold factory which cost £100,000 in June 1987. Because of mining operations nearby, part of the factory is severely damaged by subsidence and has to be demolished and rebuilt. The value of the factory after the damage is £150,000. The risk is not covered under A's insurance policy but the mining company agrees to pay compensation of £50,000 in full settlement, received in February 1998. The cost of demolition and rebuilding is £60,000, incurred in May 1998. The factory is sold in March 2007 for £300,000. The factory is a business asset throughout for taper relief purposes.

Indexation factors	June 1987 to February 1998	0.573
	June 1987 to April 1998	0.596
	February 1998 to April 1998	0.014

(i) No claim under *TCGA 1992, s 23(1)*

(*a*)   Part disposal February 1998

	£
Disposal proceeds	50,000
Deduct Allowable cost $\dfrac{50,000}{50,000 + 150,000} \times £100,000$	25,000
Unindexed gain	25,000
Indexation allowance £25,000 × 0.573	14,325
Chargeable gain 1997/98	£10,675

(*b*)   Disposal March 2006

Disposal proceeds		300,000
Deduct Allowable cost		
£(100,000 − 25,000) + £60,000		135,000
Unindexed gain		£165,000
Indexation allowance:		
original cost £(100,000 − 25,000) × 0.596	44,700	
rebuilding cost	—	44,700
Pre-tapered gain		120,300
Deduct Taper relief £120,300 × 75% (note (*a*))		90,225
Chargeable gain 2006/07		£30,075

**(ii) Claim under *TCGA 1992, s 23(1)*

			£
(a)	No chargeable gain in February 1998		
	Allowable cost		100,000
	Rebuilding cost		60,000
			160,000
	Deduct Receipt rolled over		50,000
	Revised allowable cost		£110,000
(b)	Disposal March 2007		
	Disposal proceeds		300,000
	Deduct Allowable cost		110,000
	Unindexed gain		£190,000
	Indexation allowance:		
	original cost £100,000 × 0.596	59,600	
	rebuilding cost	—	
		59,600	
	Deduct		
	Receipt rolled over £50,000 × 0.014	(700)	58,900
	Pre-tapered gain		131,100
	Deduct Taper relief £131,100 × 75% (note (a))		98,325
	Chargeable gain 2006/07		£32,775

Notes

(a)   Business asset taper relief is 75% — by reference to a qualifying holding period of two whole years or more after 5 April 1998. In practice, any losses on other 2006/07 disposals must be taken into account before taper relief is applied to the gain (see 228.1(B) TAPER RELIEF).

(b)   Note that, as well as deferring what would have been the gain on the part disposal, the effect of the claim under *TCGA 1992, s 23(1)* in this case is to increase the quantum of taper relief available on the ultimate disposal.

207   Companies

Cross-references. See also CT 104 CAPITAL GAINS.

207.1 **CAPITAL LOSSES**

P Ltd, which makes up accounts to 30 June annually, changes its accounting date to 31 December. It makes up 18-month accounts to 31 December 2006, and its chargeable gains and allowable losses are as follows

	Gains/(losses)
	£
31.7.05	4,600
19.10.05	11,500
1.12.05	3,500
28.3.06	(8,300)
21.7.06	8,500
1.9.06	(25,000)
20.12.06	7,000

The period of account is split into two accounting periods

1.7.05 – 30.6.06	
Net chargeable gain	£11,300
1.7.06 – 31.12.06	
Net allowable loss	£9,500

Notes

(*a*)   The loss cannot be set off against the £11,300 net gain in the earlier accounting period (but *can* be carried forward against subsequent gains).

(*b*)   A loss accruing to a company on a disposal on or after 5 December 2005 is not an allowable loss if it arises directly or indirectly in consequence of, or otherwise in connection with, any arrangements one of the main purposes of which is to secure a tax advantage. [*TCGA 1992, s 8(2); FA 2006, s 69*].

(*c*)   For a further example, see CT 104.1 CAPITAL GAINS.

207.2 **SHARES — ACQUISITIONS AND DISPOSALS WITHIN SHORT PERIOD** [*TCGA 1992, s 106; FA 2000, Sch 29 para 18; FA 2006, s 72(1)(3), Sch 26 Pt 3(10)*]

S Ltd has the following transactions in shares in Q plc, a quoted company with share capital of £1m divided into 25p ordinary shares.

	Date	Number of shares	Price £
Purchase	1.6.01	100,000	62,000
Purchase	1.8.05	50,000	49,000
Sale	15.8.05	80,000	60,000
Purchase	31.8.05	50,000	35,000

The position is as follows

The shares sold on 15.8.05 are identified with the two purchases on 1.8.05 and 31.8.05 (in that order).

	£

(i) Purchase on 1.8.05

	£
Proceeds $\dfrac{50,000}{80,000} \times £60,000$	37,500
Cost	49,000
Allowable loss	£11,500

(ii) Purchase on 31.8.05

	£
Proceeds $\dfrac{30,000}{80,000} \times £60,000$	22,500
Cost $\dfrac{30,000}{50,000} \times £35,000$	21,000
Chargeable gain	£1,500

Net allowable loss on transaction £10,000

Notes

(a) Where a company disposes of shares (including securities other than gilt-edged securities) before 5 December 2005 and acquires similar shares within one month before or after the disposal through a stock exchange or within six months in other circumstances, the shares acquired and disposed of are matched. For these rules to apply, the number of shares held at some time in the one month (or six months) before the disposal must be not less than 2% of the number issued. Shares acquired within one month (or six months) before or after the disposal are called 'available shares'.

(b) Subject to *TCGA 1992, s 105* (matching of same day acquisitions and disposals), disposals are identified first from 'available shares', taking acquisitions before the disposal (latest first) before acquisitions after the disposal (earliest first). Once all 'available shares' have been matched with the disposal, the identification of any remaining shares disposed of follows the ordinary rules.

207.2 Companies

(c) *TCGA 1992, s 106* is repealed with effect for disposals on or after 5 December 2005. [*FA 2006, s 72(1)(3), Sch 26 Pt 3(10)*]. It is considered to be unnecessary following the introduction of the provision mentioned in note (*b*) to 207.1 above which denies relief for losses arising from arrangements intended to secure a tax advantage and therefore provides an alternative mechanism to prevent loss creation using bed and breakfasting of shares. (Treasury Explanatory Notes to the Finance (No 2) Bill 2006).

208   Computation of Gains and Losses

208.1 ALLOWABLE AND NON-ALLOWABLE EXPENDITURE

(A) Allowable expenditure [*TCGA 1992, s 38*]

In 2006/07 T sold a house which he had owned since 1991 and which was let throughout the period of ownership (other than as furnished holiday accommodation). The house cost £34,000, with legal costs of £900, in June 1991. T spent £2,000 on initial dilapidations in July 1991. In November 1998, he added an extension at a cost of £5,500 for which he received a local authority grant of £2,500 on completion. Legal costs of £500 were incurred on obtaining vacant possession at the end of the final tenancy in May 2006. The sale proceeds were £70,000 before deducting incidental costs (including valuation fees) of £1,200. There are no other disposals in 2006/07.

			£	£	£
Indexation factors	June 1991 to April 1998 (note (*b*))			0.213	
	July 1991 to April 1998			0.215	
Sale proceeds				70,000	
Deduct Costs of sale				1,200	68,800
Cost of house				34,000	
Add Incidental costs of purchase				900	
				34,900	
Improvement costs:					
Initial dilapidations	(note (*a*))		2,000		
Extension, less grant			3,000	5,000	
Cost of obtaining vacant possession					
(enhancement cost)				500	40,400
Unindexed gain					28,400
Indexation allowance:					
£34,900 × 0.213				7,434	
£2,000 × 0.215				430	
					7,864
Pre-tapered gain					20,536
Deduct Taper relief £20,536 × 35%					
(non-business asset rate)					7,188
Chargeable gain 2006/07					£13,348

Notes

(*a*)   It is assumed that the cost of the initial dilapidations were disallowed for income tax purposes under the rule in *Law Shipping Co Ltd v CIR, CS 1923, 12 TC 621*. If any of the expenditure had been so allowed, a deduction would to that extent be precluded as an allowable deduction for CGT purposes by *TCGA 1992, s 39*.

(*b*)   Other than for the purposes of corporation tax on chargeable gains, indexation allowance is frozen at its April 1998 level and is not given at all on post-March 1998 expenditure. See 212 INDEXATION.

208.2   Computation of Gains and Losses

(B) Non-allowable expenditure — capital allowances [*TCGA 1992, s 41; FA 2000, Sch 29 para 12; CAA 2001, Sch 2 para 78*]

S Ltd acquired land in March 2001 for £90,000 on which it constructed a factory for use in its manufacturing trade. The cost of construction was £45,000 incurred in June 2001. In June 2006, the company sold the freehold factory for £140,000, of which £100,000 related to the land and £40,000 to the building. Industrial buildings allowances of £9,000 had been given and there was a balancing charge of £4,000. For the purposes of this example, it is assumed that the indexation factor for the period March 2001 to June 2006 is 0.171.

	Land	Building	
	£	£	£
Disposal consideration	100,000		40,000
Allowable cost	90,000	45,000	
Deduct net allowances given		5,000	40,000
Unindexed gain	10,000		Nil
Indexation allowance £90,000 × 0.171 = £15,390,			
but restricted to	10,000		
Chargeable gain/(allowable loss)	Nil		Nil

208.2   **PART DISPOSALS** [*TCGA 1992, s 42*]

Note. See also 215.1 LAND for small part disposals of land.

(A)

T purchased a 300-acre estate in March 1988 for £1m plus legal and other costs of £50,000. In January 1991 he spent £47,000 on improvements to the main house on the estate (not his main residence), which he sells in September 2006 for £660,000. The costs of sale are £40,000. The value of the remaining land is £2.34m. The indexation factor from March 1988 to April 1998 is 0.562, and that for January 1991 to April 1998 is 0.249.

	£	£
Sale proceeds		660,000
Deduct incidental costs		40,000
		620,000
Cost £1,050,000 × $\dfrac{660,000}{660,000 + 2,340,000}$	231,000	
Improvement costs	47,000	278,000
Unindexed gain		342,000
Indexation allowance:		
£231,000 × 0.562	129,822	
£47,000 × 0.249	11,703	141,525
Chargeable gain (subject to TAPER RELIEF (228))		£200,475

Note

(*a*)   The improvements expenditure is not apportioned as it relates entirely to the part of the estate being sold. [*TCGA 1992, s 42(4)*].

(B)

U inherited some land at a probate value of £500,000 in November 1981. Its market value at 31 March 1982 was £540,000. In November 1987, he sold part of the land for £240,000, the remaining land then being worth £480,000. He sells the remaining land in April 2006 for £600,000 and elects under *TCGA 1992, s 35(5)* for all his assets held at 31 March 1982 to be treated as sold and re-acquired by him at their market value on that date.

The gain, subject to indexation, on the part disposal in November 1987 is

	£
Proceeds	240,000
Cost £500,000 × $\dfrac{240,000}{240,000 + 480,000}$	166,667
Gain subject to indexation	£73,333

The gain, subject to indexation and taper relief, on the disposal in April 2006 is

	£
Proceeds	600,000
Market value 31.3.82	
£540,000 × $\dfrac{480,000}{240,000 + 480,000}$	360,000
Gain subject to indexation to April 1998 and taper relief	£240,000

Note

(a) Where re-basing applies and there has been a part disposal after 31 March 1982 and before 6 April 1988, the proportion of 31 March 1982 value to be brought into account on the ultimate disposal is the same as the proportion of cost unallowed on the part disposal, as if the re-basing provisions had applied to the part disposal. [*TCGA 1992, Sch 3 para 4(1)*].

208.2   Computation of Gains and Losses

(C)

V bought the film rights of a novel for £50,000 in May 1997. A one-third share of the rights was sold to W Ltd in March 1998 for £20,000, when the rights retained had a value of £45,000. In December 2006, V's rights were sold to a film company for £100,000 plus a right to royalties, such right being estimated to be worth £150,000. The indexation factor for the periods May 1997 to March 1998 and May 1997 to April 1998 are 0.025 and 0.036 respectively.

March 1998	£
Sale proceeds	20,000
Cost £50,000 × $\dfrac{20,000}{20,000 + 45,000}$	15,385
Unindexed gain	4,615
Indexation allowance £15,385 × 0.025	385
Chargeable gain 1997/98	£4,230

December 2006	£
Sale proceeds (£100,000 + £150,000)	250,000
Cost (£50,000 − £15,385)	34,615
Unindexed gain	215,385
Indexation allowance £34,615 × 0.036	1,246
Chargeable gain 2006/07 (subject to TAPER RELIEF (228))	£214,139

Note

(a)   The right to royalties is itself an asset and could be the subject of a future disposal by V. See 206.2 CAPITAL SUMS DERIVED FROM ASSETS below and, where applicable, 229 WASTING ASSETS.

(D)

C inherited land valued at £72,000 in May 1989. He granted rights of way over the land to a neighbouring landowner in March 1994, in consideration for a parcel of land adjacent to his, valued at £21,000. The value of the original land, subject to the right of way, was then £147,000. In March 2007, C sold the whole of the land for £170,000.

Indexation factors May 1989 to March 1994	0.239
May 1989 to April 1998	0.414
March 1994 to April 1998	0.141

Part disposal in March 1994		£
Disposal consideration		21,000
Allowable expenditure		
$\dfrac{21,000}{21,000 + 147,000} \times £72,000$		9,000
Unindexed gain		12,000
Indexation allowance £9,000 × 0.239		2,151
Chargeable gain 1993/94		£9,849

Disposal in March 2007		£
Disposal consideration		170,000
Deduct Original land £(72,000 − 9,000)	63,000	
Addition	21,000	84,000
Unindexed gain		86,000
Indexation allowance		
(*a*) Original land £63,000 × 0.414	26,082	
(*b*) Addition £21,000 × 0.141	2,961	
		29,043
Chargeable gain 2006/07 (subject to TAPER RELIEF (228))		£56,957

Notes

(*a*)   It is assumed that the additional land is merged with the existing land to give a single asset.

(*b*)   A claim under *TCGA 1992, s 242* (small part disposals of land — see 215.1 LAND) could not be made in respect of the March 1994 part disposal as the consideration exceeded £20,000.

209   Enterprise Investment Scheme

Cross-reference. See also IT 8.2 ENTERPRISE INVESTMENT SCHEME.

209.1   DISPOSAL OF EIS SHARES MORE THAN THREE YEARS AFTER

ISSUE [*TCGA 1992, s 150A(2)(3); ICTA 1988, s 312(1A)(a); FA 2000, Sch 17 para 6(4), para 8; SI 2005 No 3229, Reg 110*]

On 8 November 2006 P subscribes £675,000 for 450,000 shares in the EIS company, S Ltd, and obtains an EIS income tax deduction of £80,000 (£400,000 × 20%) for 2006/07. On 3 April 2011 he sells the entire holding for £1,395,000. The shares are business assets throughout for the purposes of taper relief.

The chargeable gain arising is calculated as follows

	£
Disposal proceeds	1,395,000
Cost	675,000
Gain	720,000
Less TCGA 1992, s 150A(2)(3) exemption	
£720,000 × $\dfrac{80,000}{135,000}$ (note (*b*))	426,667
Chargeable gain	293,333
Less taper relief @ 75% (note (*d*))	220,000
Taxable gain 2010/11	£73,333

Notes

(*a*) Gains arising on the sale more than three years after issue of shares qualifying for EIS income tax relief (five years for shares issued before 6 April 2000) are not chargeable gains unless the EIS relief is fully withdrawn before disposal. The exemption begins three years after the date of commencement of the qualifying trade if this is later than three years after issue.

(*b*) Where the income tax relief is not given on the full EIS subscription (otherwise than because of insufficient income), capital gains tax relief is given on a proportion of the gain on the disposal or part disposal.

The gain is reduced by the multiple A/B where

A = the actual income tax reduction and
B = the tax at the lower rate for the year of relief on the amount subscribed for the issue.

A = £400,000 × 20% = £80,000
B = £675,000 × 20% = £135,000

(*c*) Expenditure incurred after 31 March 1998 other than by companies does not attract indexation allowance. [*TCGA 1992, ss 53(1A), 54(1)(1A); FA 1998, s 121(1)–(3)*].

(*d*) Business asset taper relief is the maximum 75% — by reference to a qualifying holding period of at least two years (for disposals after 5 April 2002). In practice, any losses on other 2010/11 disposals must be taken into account before taper relief is applied to the gain (see 228.1(B) TAPER RELIEF).

209.2 **LOSS ON DISPOSAL OF EIS SHARES** [*TCGA 1992, s 150A(1)(2A)*]

(A) Disposal more than three years after issue

Assuming the facts otherwise remain the same as in 209.1 above but that the shares are sold for £450,000 on 3 April 2011.

The allowable loss arising is calculated as follows

	£	£
Disposal proceeds		450,000
Less Cost	675,000	
Less Income tax relief given (and not withdrawn)	80,000	595,000
Allowable loss 2010/11		£145,000

Note

(*a*) Any loss arising is reduced by deducting the amount of the EIS relief (given and not withdrawn) from the acquisition cost. On the question of income tax withdrawal, see note (*b*) to (B) below.

(B) Disposal within three years of issue

The facts are otherwise as in (A) above except that the shares are sold in an arm's length bargain on 3 April 2008, i.e. within three years after their issue.

Income tax relief given for 2006/07 is withdrawn as follows

Relief attributable (£400,000 @ 20%)   £80,000 (1)

$$\text{Consideration } £450,000 \times \frac{80,000 \ (£400,000 \ @ \ 20\%)}{135,000 \ (£675,000 \ @ \ 20\%)} \ @ \ 20\% \qquad £53,333 \ (2)$$

The amount at (1) is greater than that at (2), so income tax relief of £53,333 is withdrawn. [*ICTA 1988, s 299(1)–(4)*].

The relief not withdrawn is therefore £(80,000 − 53,333) =   £26,667

The allowable loss arising is calculated as follows

	£	£
Disposal proceeds		450,000
Less Cost	675,000	
Less Income tax relief not withdrawn	26,667	648,333
Allowable loss 2007/08		£198,333

Notes

(*a*) For the purposes of computing an allowable loss, the consideration is reduced by the relief attributable to the shares. [*TCGA 1992, s 150A(1)*]. The relief attributable is that remaining following any withdrawal of relief.

(*b*) A withdrawal of income tax relief arises on a disposal of EIS shares within the relevant period under *ICTA 1988, s 312(1A)(a)*, i.e. within three years after their issue or, if later, within the period ending immediately before the third anniversary of the date of commencement of the qualifying trade (within five years after issue in the case of shares issued before 6 April 2000). [*ICTA 1988, s 299(1)*].

209.3 Enterprise Investment Scheme

209.3 **EIS DEFERRAL RELIEF** [*TCGA 1992, Schs 5B, 5BA; FA 2000, Sch 17 para 7(2)(3), para 8; FA 2001, Sch 15 paras 25–37, 40*]

(A)

On 1 June 2006, X realises a gain of £300,000 (before taper relief) on the disposal of an asset. He had owned the asset since September 2004 and it had been a business asset throughout for taper relief purposes. X makes no other disposals in 2006/07. On 1 February 2008, X acquires by subscription 65% of the issued ordinary share capital of ABC Ltd at a total subscription price of £248,000. This is a qualifying investment for the purposes of EIS deferral relief, and the ABC shares are also a business asset throughout for taper relief purposes. X makes a claim to defer the maximum £248,000 of the June 2006 gain against the qualifying investment.

On 1 July 2012, X sells 40% of his holding in ABC Ltd for £199,200. He makes no other disposals in 2012/13.

X's CGT position for 2006/07 is as follows

	£
Indexed gain	300,000
Less EIS deferral relief	248,000
	52,000
Less taper relief £52,000 @ 50%	26,000
	26,000
Less annual exemption	8,800
Taxable gain 2006/07	£17,200

X's CGT position for 2012/13 is as follows

	£
Gain on ABC Ltd shares	
Disposal proceeds	199,200
Less cost (£248,000 @ 40%)	99,200
	100,000
Less taper relief £100,000 @ 75%	75,000
Chargeable gain	£25,000
Deferred gain brought into charge	
Total gain deferred	£248,000

	£
Clawback restricted to expenditure to which disposal relates	99,200
Less taper relief £99,200 @ 50%	49,600
Gain	£49,600

Taxable gains 2012/13 (subject to annual exemption) (£25,000 + £49,600)	£74,600
Gain remaining deferred until any future chargeable event (£248,000 − £99,200)	£148,800

Notes

(a) No part of X's subscription for ABC Ltd shares can qualify for EIS income tax relief. X is connected with the company by virtue of his shareholding being greater than 30%. (In practice, the holdings of his associates, e.g. wife and children, must also be taken into account in applying the 30% limit.) [*ICTA 1988, s 291(1), ss 291B, 312(1); FA 2001, Sch 15 paras 10, 40*].

(b) As the ABC Ltd shares do not qualify for income tax relief, there is no CGT exemption for the gain arising on disposal even though the shares were held for the requisite three-year period.

(c) Business asset taper relief is given by reference to the number of complete years an asset has been held after 5 April 1998. See 228 TAPER RELIEF. Taper relief on the deferred gain becoming chargeable is given by reference to the time and circumstances of the original disposal, not the disposal of the EIS shares giving rise to the chargeable event (but see (B) below re cases of serial reinvestment). [*TCGA 1992, Sch A1 para 16; FA 1998, s 121, Sch 20*].

(B) Serial reinvestment

On 1 June 2006, Anna realises a gain of £300,000 (after indexation but before taper relief) on the disposal of a complete holding of shares in ABC Ltd (an EIS company) for which she had subscribed on 1 June 2005 and in respect of which she had deferred a gain of £10,000 which would otherwise have accrued in 2003/04 on a disposal of quoted shares. The ABC Ltd shares were a business asset throughout for taper relief purposes. Anna makes no other disposals in 2006/07. On 1 December 2007, she subscribes £260,000 for new ordinary shares in a new company, EIS Ltd. The investment is a qualifying investment for the purposes of EIS deferral relief (but not income tax relief) and a business asset throughout for the purposes of taper relief. Anna makes a claim to defer the maximum £260,000 of the June 2006 gain against her investment in EIS Ltd.

On 1 June 2011, Anna sells her holding of EIS Ltd shares for £540,000. She makes no other disposals in 2011/12.

Anna's CGT position for 2006/07 is as follows

	£
Gain on ABC Ltd shares	300,000
Less deferred under EIS provisions	260,000
	40,000
Less taper relief £40,000 @ 50% (Qualifying holding period 1.6.05–1.6.06 = 1 year)	20,000
	20,000
Previously deferred gain now chargeable (note (*c*))	10,000
	30,000
Less annual exemption	8,800
Taxable gain 2006/07	£21,200

209.3 Enterprise Investment Scheme

Anna's CGT position for 2011/12 is as follows

Gain on EIS Ltd shares	£
Disposal proceeds	540,000
Less cost	260,000
	280,000
Less taper relief £280,000 @ 75% (Qualifying holding period 1.12.07 – 1.6.11 = 3 years)	210,000
Gain	£70,000

Deferred gain brought into charge	£
Gain deferred	260,000
Less taper relief @ 75%*	195,000
Gain	£65,000

*Qualifying holding period
1.6.05–1.6.06 — 1 year
1.12.07–1.6.11 — 3.5 years
Total — 4.5 years (i.e. 4 whole years)

Taxable gains 2011/12 (subject to annual exemption) (£70,000 + £65,000)	£135,000

Notes

(*a*) A special taper relief rule applies in cases of serial EIS investment. It applies in consequence of the disposal of a holding of EIS shares (the initial investment) (which were issued after 5 April 1998 and to which either CGT deferral relief or income tax relief (or both) is attributable) where the whole or part of the gain otherwise accruing is deferred by reinvestment in further EIS shares (the second investment). Upon a disposal of the second investment, with the result that the deferred gain on the initial investment is revived, taper relief is calculated in respect of the revived gain as if the holding periods of the two investments were combined. [*TCGA 1992, s 150D, Sch 5BA*]. See generally 228 TAPER RELIEF.

(*b*) Where the revived gain is itself deferred by means of a third EIS investment (not illustrated in this example), the holding periods of all three investments are combined for taper relief purposes, and so on as regards fourth and subsequent investments.

(*c*) The taper relief period for the first asset (a non-EIS investment) ends on the date of disposal of that asset (see (A) above) and does not fall to be extended under the serial reinvestment provisions. No taper relief is due in this case as the asset is a non-business asset held for less than three years after 5 April 1998.

210 Exemptions and Reliefs

Cross-references. See also 222 PRIVATE RESIDENCES, 223 QUALIFYING CORPORATE BONDS and 229 WASTING ASSETS.

210.1 CHATTELS

(A) Marginal relief [*TCGA 1992, s 262(2)*]
On 1 April 1988, Y acquired by inheritance a painting valued for probate at £900. He sold it for £7,200 on 30 October 2006, incurring costs of £150. The indexation factor for the period April 1988 to April 1998 (note (*a*)) is 0.537.

	£	£
Disposal proceeds	7,200	
Incidental costs	150	7,050
Acquisition cost		900
Unindexed gain		6,150
Indexation allowance £900 × 0.537		483
Chargeable gain		£5,667
Marginal relief		
Chargeable gain limited to $\frac{5}{3}$ × (£7,200 – £6,000)		£2,000

Notes

(*a*) Other than for the purposes of corporation tax on chargeable gains, indexation allowance is frozen at its April 1998 level. Therefore, the indexation factor for April 1998 is used in respect of disposals in a later month (and expenditure incurred in April 1998 or later does not attract indexation allowance at all). See 212 INDEXATION.

(*b*) The chargeable gain of £2,000 is subject to taper relief at the non-business asset rate of 35% (asset held eight years after 5 April 1998 plus one bonus year), reducing it to £1,300. (Any losses available must be set against gains before applying taper relief — see 228.1(B) TAPER RELIEF.).

(B) Loss relief [*TCGA 1992, s 262(3)*]
Z bought a piece of antique jewellery for £7,000 in February 1991. In January 2006, he is forced to sell it, but at auction it realises only £1,500 and Z incurs costs of £100.

	£	£
Deemed disposal consideration		6,000
Cost of disposal	100	
Cost of acquisition	7,000	7,100
Allowable loss		£1,100

Note

(*a*) Where the disposal consideration for tangible movable property is less than £6,000 and there would otherwise be a loss, the consideration is deemed to be £6,000.

(C) Partial disposal of assets forming sets [*TCGA 1992, s 262(4)*]
AB purchased a set of six 18th century dining chairs in 1979 for £1,200. After incurring restoration costs of £300 in 1981, he sold two of them in May 2002 to an unconnected person for £2,900. In October 2006, he sold the other four to the same buyer for £4,900. The value of the complete set at 31 March 1982 was £1,800.

Indexation factor	March 1982 to April 1998 (note (*c*))	1.047

The two disposals are treated as one for the purposes of the chattel exemption and marginal relief, the consideration for which is £7,800. Marginal relief on this basis would give a total chargeable gain of £3,000 ([£7,800 − £6,000] × $\frac{5}{3}$) which is to be compared with the following:

May 2002	£	£	£
Disposal proceeds		2,900	2,900
Acquisition cost	1,200		
Enhancement cost	300		
	1,500		
Cost of two chairs sold £1,500 × $\frac{2}{6}$		500	
Market value 31.3.82 £1,800 × $\frac{2}{6}$			600
Unindexed gain		2,400	2,300
Indexation allowance £600 × 1.047		628	628
Gain after indexation		£1,772	£1,672
Chargeable gain			£1,672

October 2006		£	£
Disposal proceeds		4,900	4,900
Allowable cost £1,500 × $\frac{4}{6}$		1,000	
Market value 31.3.82 £1,800 × $\frac{4}{6}$			1,200
Unindexed gain		3,900	3,700
Indexation allowance £1,200 × 1.047		1,256	1,256
Gain after indexation		£2,644	£2,444
Chargeable gain			£2,444

Total chargeable gains (£1,672 + £2,444)	£4,116

The total gain of £4,116 compares with a gain of £3,000 using marginal relief. Marginal relief is therefore effective and the total chargeable gain is £3,000.

The gain is apportioned to tax years as follows (note (*b*))

2002/03 £3,000 × $\dfrac{2,900}{7,800}$ =   £1,115

2006/07 £3,000 × $\dfrac{4,900}{7,800}$ =   £1,885

Notes

(*a*)   Prior to the second disposal, the first disposal would have been exempt, the proceeds being within the £6,000 chattel exemption.

(*b*)   The gain as reduced by marginal relief is apportioned between tax years in the same ratio as the proportion of total sale proceeds applicable to each year (HMRC Capital Gains Manual, CG 76637).

(*c*)   Other than for the purposes of corporation tax on chargeable gains, indexation allowance is frozen at its April 1998 level. Therefore, the indexation factor for April 1998 is used in respect of disposals in a later month (and expenditure incurred in April 1998 or later does not attract indexation allowance at all). See 212 INDEXATION.

(*d*)   The gains are subject to TAPER RELIEF (228).

(*e*)   See also 202.4 ANTI-AVOIDANCE.

211   Hold-Over Reliefs

211.1 **RELIEF FOR GIFTS** [*TCGA 1992, s 260*]

(A) Chargeable lifetime transfers

B owns a house which he has not occupied as a private residence. He purchased the house for £15,200 inclusive of costs in 1979 and in January 2007 he gives it to a discretionary trust of which he is the settlor. The settlement is not a settlor-interested settlement for the purposes of *TCGA 1992, ss 169B–169G*. The market value of the house is agreed to be £60,000 at the date of transfer, and B incurs transfer costs of £1,000. The indexation factor for the period March 1982 to April 1998 (note (*c*)) is 1.047. The house had a value of £21,000 at 31 March 1982.

	£	£
Disposal consideration	60,000	60,000
Deduct Costs of disposal	1,000	1,000
	59,000	59,000
Cost	15,200	
Market value 31.3.82		21,000
Unindexed gain	43,800	38,000
Indexation allowance £21,000 × 1.047	21,987	21,987
Gain after indexation	£21,813	£16,013
Chargeable gain (subject to TAPER RELIEF (228))		£16,013

If B elects under *TCGA 1992, s 260*, his chargeable gain is reduced to nil, and the trustees' acquisition cost of the house is treated as £43,987 (£60,000 – £16,013). No taper relief is then due (note (*d*)).

Notes

(*a*)   Relief under *TCGA 1992, s 260* is restricted, generally, to transfers which are, or would but for annual exemptions be, chargeable lifetime transfers for inheritance tax purposes.

(*b*)   There are special rules where deferral took place after 31 March 1982 but before 6 April 1988, for which see 205.2 ASSETS HELD ON 31 MARCH 1982.

(*c*)   Other than for the purposes of corporation tax on chargeable gains, indexation allowance is frozen at its April 1998 level. Therefore, the indexation factor for April 1998 is used in respect of disposals in a later month (and expenditure incurred in April 1998 or later does not attract indexation allowance at all). See 212 INDEXATION.

(*d*)   A held-over gain cannot attract taper relief. On a future disposal by the donee, any gain will be tapered by reference only to the donee's period of ownership.

(*e*)   Separate rules apply to transfers of assets between MARRIED PERSONS AND CIVIL PARTNERS (217).

(*f*)   Relief under *TCGA 1992, s 260* is not available on a disposal after 9 December 2003 to the trustees of a settlor-interested settlement (as defined). [*TCGA 1992, ss 169B–169G; FA 2004, s 116, Sch 21*].

(B) Disposal consideration [*TCGA 1992, s 260(5)*]
The facts are as in (A) above except that B sells the house to the trustees for £30,000.

	£	£
Chargeable gain (as above) (note (*a*))		16,013
Deduct		
Actual consideration passing	30,000	
B's allowable costs (note (*b*))	(22,000)	
		8,000
Held-over gain		£8,013

(i)	B's chargeable gain is reduced to £16,013 − £8,013	£8,000
(ii)	The trustees' allowable cost is reduced to £60,000 − £8,013	£51,987

Notes
(*a*)   The disposal consideration is taken as the open market value of the house at the date of disposal because B and the trustees are connected persons. Thus, the computation of the gain is as in (A) above.

(*b*)   B's allowable costs are those allowable under *TCGA 1992, s 38* (costs of acquisition and disposal), which do not include indexation allowance.

(C) Relief for IHT [*TCGA 1992, s 260(7)*]
The facts are as in (A) above. Before transferring the house, B had made substantial chargeable transfers. Inheritance tax of £12,000 is payable on the transfer. The trustees sell the house in December 2007 for £55,000.

	£	£
Disposal proceeds		55,000
Acquisition cost	60,000	
Deduct held-over gain	16,013	
		43,987
Gain		11,013
IHT attributable to earlier transfer (restricted)		11,013
Chargeable gain		Nil

Notes
(*a*)   The IHT deduction is limited to the amount of the gain and cannot create or increase a loss. [*TCGA 1992, s 260(7)*].

(*b*)   A similar inheritance tax relief operates where the original gain was held over under *TCGA 1992, s 165* or *FA 1980, s 79*. [*TCGA 1992, ss 67, 165(10)*].

(*c*)   Expenditure incurred (or deemed to be incurred) in April 1998 or later (other than by companies) does not attract indexation allowance. [*TCGA 1992, s 53(1A), s 54(1A); FA 1998, s 122(1)–(3)*].

211.2   Hold-Over Reliefs

211.2 **RELIEF FOR GIFTS OF BUSINESS ASSETS** [*TCGA 1992, s 165, Sch 7*]

Zoë owns a freehold property which she lets to the family trading company, Sphere Ltd, in which she and her father each own half the shares and voting rights. Zoë inherited the property in April 1990 at a probate value of £50,000, and since then the whole of the property has been used for the purposes of the company's trade. In November 2006, Zoë transfers the property to her boyfriend. Its market value at that time is £115,000. The intention is that he should give sufficient consideration to leave Zoë with a chargeable gain exactly equal to the annual exempt amount (there being no other disposals in 2006/07). The indexation factor for the period April 1990 to April 1998 is 0.300.

Actual consideration should be £85,200 as shown by the following computation

	£	£
Deemed consideration		115,000
Deduct: Cost	50,000	
Indexation allowance £50,000 × 0.300	15,000	65,000
Unrelieved gain		50,000
Held-over gain (see below)		14,800
Pre-tapered gain		35,200
Taper relief £35,200 × 75%		
(business asset held at least 2 years)		26,400
Chargeable gain covered by annual exemption		£8,800

Computation of held-over gain	£	£
Unrelieved gain		50,000
Actual consideration	85,200	
Less allowable expenditure (excluding indexation)	50,000	35,200
Held-over gain		£14,800

Notes

(*a*)   On a subsequent disposal of the property, the allowable expenditure would be £100,200 (deemed proceeds of £115,000 less held-over gain of £14,800). The actual consideration given does not enter into this calculation. No indexation allowance will be due as the expenditure was incurred after March 1998 (see 212 INDEXATION).

(*b*)   If no part of the unrelieved gain were held over, business asset taper relief of 75% would have been available on the full amount. As a result of the hold-over claim, taper relief is forgone on the amount held over, and the transferee does not inherit the transferor's period of ownership. The availability and quantum of taper relief need to be taken into account in the decision-making. See 228 TAPER RELIEF. One consideration is whether the transferee's period of ownership and use of the asset are expected to be such as to obtain the maximum potential taper relief.

211.3 TRANSFER OF BUSINESS TO A COMPANY

(A) Incorporation relief [*TCGA 1992, s 162*]

W carries on an antiquarian bookselling business. He decides to form an unquoted company, P Ltd, to carry on the business. He transfers, in August 2006, the whole of the business undertaking, assets and liabilities to P Ltd, in consideration for the issue of shares, plus an amount left outstanding on interest-free loan. The business assets and liabilities transferred are valued as follows

		Value	Chargeable gain (after indexation to April 1998)
	£	£	£
Freehold shop premises (acquired in 1990)		80,000	52,000
Goodwill		36,000	26,000
Fixtures and fittings		4,000	—
Trading stock		52,000	—
Debtors		28,000	—
		200,000	
Mortgage on shop	50,000		
Trade creditors	20,000	70,000	—
		£130,000	£78,000

The company issues 100,000 £1 ordinary shares, valued at par, to W in August 2006, and the amount left outstanding is £30,000. W does not elect to disapply incorporation relief. In March 2007, W sells 20,000 of his shares for £45,000 to X. W's remaining shareholding is then worth, say, £155,000.

(i) Amount of chargeable gain rolled over on transfer of the business

$$\frac{100,000}{130,000} \times £78,000 \qquad\qquad £60,000$$

Of the chargeable gain, £18,000 (£78,000 − £60,000) remains taxable, but is subject to taper relief at 75%, reducing it to £4,500 (see note (*b*)).

The allowable cost of W's shares is £40,000 (£100,000 − £60,000).

(ii) On the sale of shares to X, W realises a chargeable gain

	£
Disposal consideration	45,000
Allowable cost £40,000 $\times \dfrac{45,000}{45,000 + 155,000}$	9,000
Chargeable gain (no taper relief as shares held less than 12 months)	£36,000

Notes

(*a*)   Relief under *TCGA 1992, s 162* is given automatically and without the need for a claim (but see (B) below).

(*b*)   Where part of the aggregate chargeable gain on the old assets remains in charge, after giving relief under *TCGA 1992, s 162*, HMRC will accept a computation of taper relief on this amount by reference to the holding period(s) of *any* of the *chargeable* assets transferred (HMRC Capital Gains Manual CG 65821, 65826).

211.3 Hold-Over Reliefs

The shop premises have been held by W for at least two years after 5 April 1998, and thus the whole gain qualifies at 75%.

(c) In the hands of the company, the goodwill will not qualify for the special treatment of intangible assets of companies introduced by *FA 2002, s 84, Sch 29*, because it was acquired from a related party and was created before 1 April 2002 (by virtue of the business having been carried on before that date). [*FA 2002, Sch 29 paras 95, 117, 118, 121*].

(d) See 205.2 ASSETS HELD ON 31 MARCH 1982 for the relief given under *TCGA 1992, Sch 4* where gains were held over after 31 March 1982 and before 6 April 1988 and a disposal occurs after 5 April 1988. This relief applies, inter alia, to gains held over under the rules illustrated above.

(B) Election to disapply incorporation relief [*TCGA 1992, s 162A; FA 2002, s 49*]
The facts are as in (A) above, except that W considers an election under *TCGA 1992, s162A* to disapply *TCGA 1992, s 162*. With an election, the computations in (A) are revised as follows.

(i) Chargeable gain on transfer of the business

	£
Gain after indexation but before taper relief	78,000
Less Taper relief £78,000 @ 75% (asset held at least 2 years)	58,500
Chargeable gain	£19,500

(ii) Chargeable gain on sale of shares

	£
Disposal consideration	45,000
Allowable cost $£100,000 \times \dfrac{45,000}{45,000 + 155,000}$	22,500
Chargeable gain (no taper relief as shares held less than 12 months)	£22,500

On the face of it, the election is not beneficial, producing aggregate gains of £42,000 (£19,500 + £22,500) as against £40,500 (£4,500 + £36,000) in (A) above.

If, however, W then sells his remaining 80,000 shares for £155,000 in, say, May 2007, he will have, as illustrated below, a chargeable gain for 2007/08 of £124,000 without the election or £77,500 with the election. There is now an overall saving of £45,000 if the election is made; this is the benefit of the increased taper relief on the disposal to the company (i.e. £60,000 @ 75% = £45,000). If W had retained the shares for at least one year, such that 50% taper relief would have been available on sale, the overall saving with an election would have been reduced accordingly. See also note (b).

Chargeable gain on sale of 80,000 shares in May 2007

Without the election

	£
Disposal consideration	155,000
Allowable cost (£40,000 – £9,000)	31,000
Chargeable gain (no taper relief as shares held less than 12 months)	£124,000

With the election

	£
Disposal consideration	155,000
Allowable cost (£100,000 – £22,500)	77,500
Chargeable gain (no taper relief as shares held less than 12 months)	£77,500

Notes

(*a*)   On a transfer (of a business) that is otherwise within the scope of *TCGA 1992, s 162* at (A) above and takes place after 5 April 2002, the transferor may make an election under *TCGA 1992, s 162A* to forgo incorporation relief.

(*b*)   If instead of making the early sales illustrated in this example, W had retained all 100,000 shares for two years, such that the gain on eventual disposal would have qualified for the maximum 75% business asset taper relief, the election would have been neutral. This is because the taper relief forgone on incorporation (i.e. without an election) would have been fully recovered. (This does assume that the shares retain their status as business assets for taper relief purposes throughout W's ownership.)

212   Indexation

Cross-references. See 226.9 SHARES AND SECURITIES for indexation on a building society share account where cash bonus received on takeover or conversion, 227 SHARES AND SECURITIES — IDENTIFICATION RULES.

212.1 INDEXATION ALLOWANCE — GENERAL RULES [*TCGA 1992, ss 53–56*]

(A) Calculation of indexation factor — companies

M Ltd bought a freehold factory in December 1984 for £500,000. Further buildings are erected at a cost of £200,000 in May 1992. In May 2006 the factory is sold for £2m. The retail price index (RPI) was re-based in January 1987 from 394.5 to 100 and the relevant values are as follows

December	1984	358.5
May	1992	139.3
May	2006	197.7

	£	£
Disposal consideration		2,000,000
Deduct Cost of factory and site	500,000	
Cost of additions	200,000	700,000
Unindexed gain		1,300,000
Indexation allowance		

(i)   Factory and site
Indexation factor

$$\left(\frac{394.5 \times 197.7}{358.5} \right) - 100 = 117.6\%$$

Indexed rise
£500,000 × 1.176

	588,000	

(ii)   Additions
Indexation factor

$$\frac{197.7 - 139.3}{139.3} = 0.419$$

Indexed rise
£200,000 × 0.419

	£	£
	83,800	671,800
Gain chargeable to corporation tax		£628,200

Note

(*a*)   Alternatively the indexation factor on the pre-January 1987 expenditure can be calculated using the revised RPI figures so that, for example,

December 1984	=	90.87
May 2006	=	197.7

Indexation from December 1984 to May 2006 = $\dfrac{197.7 - 90.87}{90.87} = 1.176$

(B) Calculation of indexation factor — individuals etc.
All the facts are as in (A) above except that M is an individual rather than a company. Additional information: the value of the RPI for April 1998 (see note (*a*)) was 162.6, and the factory is a business asset throughout for taper relief purposes.

	£	£
Disposal consideration (May 2006)		2,000,000
Deduct Expenditure (December 1984)	500,000	
Expenditure (May 1992)	200,000	700,000
Unindexed gain		1,300,000
Indexation allowance		
(i) Expenditure (December 1984)		
Indexation factor		

$$\frac{162.6 - 90.87}{90.87} = 0.789$$

	£	£
Indexed rise		
£500,000 × 0.789	394,500	
(ii) Expenditure (May 1991)		
Indexation factor		

$$\frac{162.6 - 139.3}{139.3} = 0.167$$

	£	£
Indexed rise		
£200,000 × 0.167	33,400	427,900
Gain		872,100
Deduct Taper relief (£872,100 × 75%)		654,075
Chargeable gain 2006/07		£218,025

Notes

(*a*)   For individuals, trustees and personal representatives (but not for companies), indexation allowance is frozen at its April 1998 level. Therefore, the indexation factor for April 1998 is used in respect of disposals in a later month (and expenditure incurred in April 1998 or later does not attract indexation allowance at all). [*TCGA 1992, s 53(1A), s 54(1A); FA 1998, s 122(1)–(3)*].

(*b*)   Business asset taper relief is given by reference to the number of complete years an asset has been held after 5 April 1998. See 228 TAPER RELIEF. Taper relief is applied to the otherwise chargeable gain (*after* indexation to April 1998).

(*c*)   In practice, any losses on other 2006/07 disposals must be taken into account before taper relief is applied to the net gain (see 228.1(B) TAPER RELIEF).

212.1 Indexation

(C) Disposal of asset held on 31 March 1982

X acquired an antique for £6,000 in August 1979. He sold it for £17,000 in December 2006. The agreed market value of the clock at 31 March 1982 is £7,500. The indexation factor for March 1982 to April 1998 (see note (a) to (B) above) is 1.047.

	£	£
Disposal consideration	17,000	17,000
Deduct Cost	6,000	
Market value 31.3.82		7,500
Unindexed gain	11,000	9,500
Indexation allowance £7,500 × 1.047	7,853	7,853
Gain after indexation	£3,147	£1,647
Chargeable gain (subject to TAPER RELIEF (228))		£1,647

Notes

(a)   In both the calculation using cost and that using 31 March 1982 value, indexation is automatically based on 31 March 1982 value. If, however, a greater allowance would have been produced by basing indexation on cost, that would automatically have applied instead. If, however, an irrevocable election were to be made under *TCGA 1992, s 35(5)* for all assets to be treated as sold and re-acquired at 31 March 1982, indexation must then be based on 31 March 1982 value whether it is beneficial or not. [*TCGA 1992, s 55(1)(2)*].

(b)   See also 205.1 ASSETS HELD ON 31 MARCH 1982.

(D) Losses — indexation allowance restriction [*TCGA 1992, s 53(1)(b)(2A); FA 1994, s 93(1)–(3)(11)*]

In June 1990, M had purchased two paintings, each for £25,000. In September 2006, he sells the paintings for £30,000 (A) and £23,000 (B) respectively. Incidental costs of purchase and sale are ignored for the purposes of this example. The indexation factor for the period June 1990 to April 1998 (see note (a) to (B) above) is 0.283.

The gains/losses on the sales are as follows

	(A) £	(B) £
Proceeds	30,000	23,000
Cost	25,000	25,000
Unindexed gain/(loss)	5,000	(2,000)
Indexation allowance £25,000 × 0.283 = £7,075 but restricted to	(5,000)	Nil
Chargeable gain/(allowable loss)	Nil	£(2,000)

Note

(a)   Indexation allowance can reduce an unindexed gain to nil but cannot create or increase a loss.

212.2 NO GAIN/NO LOSS TRANSFERS

(A) Transfers between spouses or civil partners — asset acquired by first spouse before 1 April 1982 — no indexation allowance restriction on ultimate disposal
[*TCGA 1992, s 55(5)(6), s 56(2), s 58; SI 2005 No 3229, Reg 107*]
Mr N inherited a country cottage in 1977 at a probate value of £12,000. Its market value at 31 March 1982 was £30,000. In July 1988, Mr N incurred enhancement expenditure of £5,000 on the cottage. In May 1990, he gave the cottage to his wife. In November 2006, Mrs N sells it for £85,000. At no time was the cottage the main residence of either spouse. The relevant indexation factors are as follows

March 1982 to May 1990	0.589
July 1988 to May 1990	0.183
March 1982 to April 1998 (note (*d*))	1.047
July 1988 to April 1998 (note (*d*))	0.524

(i) Disposal in May 1990
Consideration deemed to be such that neither gain nor loss arises.

	£	£
Cost of cottage to Mr N		12,000
Enhancement expenditure		5,000
		17,000
Indexation allowance:		
£30,000 × 0.589	17,670	
£5,000 × 0.183	915	18,585
Cost of cottage to Mrs N		£35,585

(ii) Disposal in November 2006

	£	£	£
Sale proceeds		85,000	85,000
Cost	35,585		
Deduct Indexation allowance previously given	18,585		
	17,000		
Deduct Enhancement expenditure	5,000	(12,000)	
Market value 31.3.82			(30,000)
Enhancement expenditure (July 1988)		(5,000)	(5,000)
Unindexed gain		68,000	50,000
Indexation allowance:			
£30,000 × 1.047		(31,410)	(31,410)
£5,000 × 0.524		(2,620)	(2,620)
Gain after indexation		£33,970	£15,970
Chargeable gain 2006/07 (subject to TAPER RELIEF (228))			£15,970

Notes
(*a*)   Having acquired the asset by means of a no gain/no loss disposal, under *CGTA 1979, s 44* (now *TCGA 1992, s 58*), from her husband, who held it at 31 March 1982, Mrs N is deemed to have held the asset at 31 March 1982 for the purpose of the re-basing provisions, and also the provisions under which indexation allowance

is computed using value at 31 March 1982. [*TCGA 1992, s 55(5)(6), Sch 3 para 1*].

(*b*) Where for re-basing/indexation purposes a person is deemed to have held an asset at 31 March 1982, that person can also be treated as having incurred enhancement expenditure which was in fact incurred after that date by a previous holder of the asset. (Revenue Tax Bulletin August 1992 p 32).

(*c*) Re-basing does not apply to the no gain/no loss disposal. [*TCGA 1992, s 35(3)(d)(i)*].

(*d*) With effect from 5 December 2005, these provisions apply equally to transfers between same-sex partners in a civil partnership. [*SI 2005 No 3229, Reg 107*].

(*e*) Other than for the purposes of corporation tax on chargeable gains, indexation allowance is frozen at its April 1998 level. Therefore, the indexation factor for April 1998 is used in respect of disposals in a later month (and expenditure incurred in April 1998 or later does not attract indexation allowance at all). See 212.1(B) above.

(*f*) See also (B)–(D) below and 217 MARRIED PERSONS AND CIVIL PARTNERS.

(B) Transfers between spouses or civil partners — asset acquired by first spouse after 31 March 1982 — gain on ultimate disposal [*TCGA 1992, s 56(2)*]
The facts are as in (A) above except that Mr N inherited the cottage in April 1982 at a probate value of £30,000. The relevant indexation factors are

April 1982 to May 1990	0.557
July 1988 to May 1990	0.183
May 1990 to April 1998	0.288

(i) Disposal in May 1990
Consideration deemed to be such that neither gain nor loss arises.

	£	£
Cost of cottage to Mr N		30,000
Enhancement expenditure		5,000
		35,000
Indexation allowance:		
£30,000 × 0.557	16,710	
£5,000 × 0.183	915	17,625
Cost of cottage to Mrs N		£52,625

(ii) Disposal in November 2006

	£
Sale proceeds	85,000
Cost (as above)	52,625
Unindexed gain	32,375
Indexation allowance £52,625 × 0.288	15,156
Chargeable gain 2006/07 (subject to TAPER RELIEF (226))	£17,219

Note
(*a*) For further examples on transfers between spouses or civil partners, see (A) above and 217 MARRIED PERSONS AND CIVIL PARTNERS. The principles in (C) and (D) below

also apply to transfers between spouses or civil partners (except that, for such transfers, indexation allowance cannot be computed beyond April 1998 — see note (*e*) to (A) above).

(C) Intra-group transfers — asset acquired by group before 1 April 1982 — indexation allowance restricted on ultimate disposal [*TCGA 1992, s 55(5)–(9), s 56(2), s 171*]

J Ltd and K Ltd are 75% subsidiaries of H Ltd. J Ltd acquired a property in 1980 for £20,000. Its market value at 31 March 1982 was £25,000. In May 1990, J Ltd transferred the property to K Ltd. In May 2006, K Ltd sells the property outside the group. The sale proceeds are (1) £18,000 or (2) £29,000. The relevant indexation factors are as follows

March 1982 to May 1990	0.589
March 1982 to May 2006	1.489

(i) Disposal in May 1990

Consideration deemed to be such that neither gain nor loss arises.

	£
Cost of asset to J Ltd	20,000
Indexation allowance £25,000 × 0.589	14,725
Cost of asset to K Ltd	£34,725

(ii) Disposal in May 2006

(1) Proceeds £18,000

	£	£	£
Proceeds		18,000	18,000
Cost	34,725		
Deduct Indexation allowance previously given	14,725	(20,000)	
Market value 31.3.82			(25,000)
		(2,000)	(7,000)
Add Rolled-up indexation		(14,725)	(14,725)
Loss after rolled-up indexation		£(16,725)	£(21,725)
Allowable loss		£16,725	

67

212.2 Indexation

(2) Proceeds £29,000

	£	£	£
Proceeds		29,000	29,000
Cost	34,725		
Deduct Indexation allowance			
previously given	14,725		
	———	(20,000)	
Market value 31.3.82			(25,000)
Unindexed gain		9,000	4,000
Indexation allowance:			
£25,000 × 1.489 = £37,225 but restricted to		(9,000)	(4,000)
		———	———
		Nil	Nil
Excess of rolled-up indexation (£14,725)			
over indexation allowance given above		(5,725)	(10,725)
		———	———
Loss after rolled-up indexation		£(5,725)	£(10,725)
		———	———
Allowable loss		£5,725	
		———	

Notes

(*a*)   The calculation first follows that in (A) above. [*TCGA 1992, s 55(5)(6)*]. As the ultimate disposal is after 29 November 1993 and indexation allowance is either unavailable as in (1) above or restricted as in (2) above, special provisions enable the person making the disposal to obtain the benefit of any indexation allowance already accrued on no gain/no loss transfers made *before* 30 November 1993 (called 'rolled-up indexation'). [*TCGA 1992, s 55(7)–(9)*].

(*b*)   The principles illustrated in this example apply equally to inter-spouse transfers (except that, for inter-spouse transfers, indexation allowance cannot be computed beyond April 1998 — see note (*e*) to (A) above).

(D) Intra-group transfers — asset acquired by group after 31 March 1982 — loss on ultimate disposal [*TCGA 1992, s 56(2)–(4), s 171*]

L Ltd, M Ltd and N Ltd are members of a 75% group of companies. L Ltd acquired a property in June 1990 for £50,000 and transferred it to M Ltd in June 1993. M Ltd transferred the property to N Ltd in June 1996, and N Ltd sold it outside the group in June 2006 for £55,000. The relevant indexation factors are as follows

June 1990 to June 1993	0.113
June 1993 to June 1996	0.085

(i) Disposal in June 1993
Consideration deemed to be such that neither gain nor loss arises.

	£
Cost of asset to L Ltd	50,000
Indexation allowance £50,000 × 0.113	5,650
Cost of asset to M Ltd	£55,650

(ii) Disposal in June 1996
Cost of asset to M Ltd	55,650
Indexation allowance £55,650 × 0.085	4,730
Cost of asset to N Ltd	£60,380

(iii) Disposal in June 2006
Proceeds	55,000
Cost (as above)	60,380
Loss before adjustment under *TCGA 1992, s 56(3)*	5,380
Deduct Indexation on June 1996 disposal	4,730
Allowable loss	£650

Notes

(*a*)   Where a loss accrues on the ultimate disposal, it is reduced by any indexation allowance included in the cost of the asset by virtue of a no gain/no loss disposal made *after* 29 November 1993. If this adjustment would otherwise convert a loss into a gain, the disposal is treated as giving rise to neither a gain nor a loss. [*TCGA 1992, s 56(3)*].

(*b*)   The principles illustrated in this example apply equally to inter-spouse transfers (except that, for inter-spouse transfers, indexation allowance cannot be computed beyond April 1998 — see note (*e*) to (A) above).

213 Interest on Overpaid Tax

213.1 **SELF-ASSESSMENT** [*TCGA 1992, s 283*]

M's tax return for 2004/05 included a chargeable gain of £53,900 on the sale of some unquoted shares. His self-assessment showed capital gains tax payable of £18,280, i.e. £53,900 − £8,200 (annual exemption) = £45,700 @ 40% (M's marginal rate of income tax). M submitted the return and paid the tax on 27 January 2006. However, the computation included an estimated valuation of the shares as at 31 March 1982 and, following negotiations, the value was finally agreed at a figure in excess of M's estimate, resulting in a reduction of £8,000 in the chargeable gain. Thus, tax of £3,200 (£8,000 @ 40%) became repayable to M, and repayment was duly made on 9 August 2006.

The rate of interest on overpaid capital gains tax remained at 2.25% p.a. from 6 September 2005.

Repayment supplement is as follows

27.1.06 − 9.8.06 £3,200 × 2.25% × $\frac{194}{365}$	£38.27

Note

(*a*) Supplement runs from the date the tax was paid (even if before the due date — 31 January 2006 in this case) to the date the repayment order is issued, though it should be noted that HMRC do not pay supplement on any amount deliberately overpaid (Revenue Press Release 12 November 1996).

214   Interest and Surcharges on Unpaid Tax

214.1 **SELF-ASSESSMENT** [*TMA 1970, ss 59C, 86*]

Mr Watson's 2004/05 capital gains tax liability as shown in his self-assessment amounts to £5,000. On 1 June 2006 Mr Watson pays £2,000 and on 3 August 2006 he pays the £3,000 balance.

The rate of interest on overdue capital gains tax remained at 6.5% p.a. from 6 September 2005 to 5 September 2006. *Purely for illustration purposes*, it is assumed that it was decreased to 5.5% from 6 May 2006.

Mr Watson will be charged as follows

Interest and Surcharge due

	£	£
Interest		
£2,000 × 6.5% × $\frac{95}{365}$ (31.1.06 – 5.5.06)	33.83	
£2,000 × 5.5% × $\frac{26}{365}$ (6.5.06 – 1.6.06)	7.84	41.67
£3,000 × 6.5% × $\frac{95}{365}$ (31.1.06 – 5.5.06)	50.57	
£3,000 × 5.5% × $\frac{89}{365}$ (6.5.06 – 3.8.06)	40.23	90.98
		£132.65
Surcharge		
Initial surcharge — £5,000 × 5%		250.00
Additional surcharge — £3,000 × 5%		150.00
		£400.00

Notes

(*a*)   Capital gains tax is normally due on 31 January following the year of assessment. [*TMA 1970, s 59B(4)*].

(*b*)   If any tax is paid more than 28 days late, a 5% surcharge is levied in addition to interest. An additional surcharge is also levied on tax outstanding for more than six months. On appeal, surcharges may be set aside if the Commissioners accept that the taxpayer had a 'reasonable excuse' for late payment. Interest is chargeable on a surcharge and accrues from a date which is 30 days after the surcharge is imposed. [*TMA 1970, s 59C*].

215 Land

215.1 **SMALL PART DISPOSALS** [*TCGA 1992, s 242*]

C owns farmland which cost £134,000 in May 1988 and which is a business asset throughout for the purposes of TAPER RELIEF (228). In February 1996, a small plot of land is exchanged with an adjoining landowner for another piece of land. The value placed on the transaction is £18,000. The value of the remaining estate excluding the new piece of land is estimated at £250,000. In March 2007, C sells the whole estate for £300,000. He makes no other disposals in 2005/06.

Indexation factors	May 1988 to February 1996	0.421
	February 1996 to April 1998 (note (*e*))	0.078
	May 1988 to April 1998 (note (*e*))	0.531

(i) No claim made under *TCGA 1992, s 242(2)*

		£	£
(*a*)	*Disposal in February 1996*		
	Disposal proceeds		18,000
	Allowable cost $\dfrac{18,000}{18,000 + 250,000} \times £134,000$		9,000
	Unindexed gain		9,000
	Indexation allowance £9,000 × 0.421		3,789
	Chargeable gain 1995/96		£5,211
(*b*)	*Disposal in March 2007*		
	Disposal proceeds		300,000
	Allowable cost		
	Original land £(134,000 − 9,000)	125,000	
	Exchanged land	18,000	143,000
	Unindexed gain		157,000
	Indexation allowance		
	Original land £125,000 × 0.531	66,375	
	Exchanged land £18,000 × 0.078	1,404	67,779
	Pre-tapered gain		89,221
	Business asset taper relief @ 75%		66,916
	Chargeable gain 2006/07		£22,305

(ii) Claim made under *TCGA 1992, s 242(2)*

		£
(*a*)	*No disposal in February 1996*	
	Allowable cost of original land	134,000
	Deduct Disposal proceeds	18,000
	Adjusted allowable cost	£116,000
	Allowable cost of additional land	£18,000

	£	£
(b) *Disposal in March 2007*		
Disposal proceeds		300,000
Allowable cost		
Original land	116,000	
Additional land	18,000	134,000
Unindexed gain		166,000
Indexation allowance		
Original land £134,000 × 0.531	71,154	
Additional land £18,000 × 0.078	1,404	
	72,558	
Receipt set-off £18,000 × 0.078	1,404	71,154
Pre-tapered gain		94,846
Business asset taper relief @ 75%		71,135
Chargeable gain 2006/07		£23,711

Notes

(a) A claim under *TCGA 1992, s 242* may be made where the consideration for the part disposal does not exceed one-fifth of the value of the whole, up to a maximum of £20,000.

(b) If the second disposal had also been made in 1995/96 no claim under *section 242(2)* could have been made on the part disposal as proceeds of all disposals of land in the year would have exceeded £20,000.

(c) Although (ii) above gives the lower overall gain, (i) above would be preferable if there are little or no other gains for 1995/96, such that the 1995/96 gain in (i) above is fully covered by the annual exemption for that year.

(d) If the original land had been held at 31 March 1982 and the part disposal took place after that date, the disposal proceeds, on a claim under *section 242(2)*, would be deducted from the 31 March 1982 value for the purpose of the re-basing provisions.

(e) Other than for the purposes of corporation tax on chargeable gains, indexation allowance is frozen at its April 1998 level. Therefore, the indexation factor for April 1998 is used in respect of disposals in a later month (and expenditure incurred in April 1998 or later does not attract indexation allowance at all). See 212 INDEXATION.

215.2 Land

215.2 **COMPULSORY PURCHASE** [*TCGA 1992, ss 243–248*]

(A) Rollover where new land acquired

(i) Rollover not claimed

D owns freehold land purchased for £77,000 in 1978. Part of the land is made the subject of a compulsory purchase order. The compensation of £70,000 is agreed on 10 August 2006. The market value of the remaining land is £175,000. The value of the total freehold land at 31 March 1982 was £98,000. The indexation factor for the period March 1982 to April 1998 is 1.047.

	£	£
Disposal consideration	70,000	70,000
Cost £77,000 × $\dfrac{70,000}{70,000 + 175,000}$	22,000	
Market value 31.3.82		
£98,000 × $\dfrac{70,000}{70,000 + 175,000}$		28,000
Unindexed gain	48,000	42,000
Indexation allowance £28,000 × 1.047	29,316	29,316
Gain after indexation	£18,684	£12,684
Chargeable gain 2006/07 (subject to TAPER RELIEF (228))		£12,684

(ii) Rollover claimed under *TCGA 1992, s 247*

If, in (i), D acquires new land costing, say, £80,000 in, say, December 2006, relief may be claimed as follows.

	£
Allowable cost of land compulsorily purchased	28,000
Indexation allowance	29,316
Deemed consideration for disposal	57,316
Actual consideration	70,000
Chargeable gain rolled over	£12,684
Allowable cost of new land (£80,000 − £12,684)	£67,316

(B) Small disposals

(i) No rollover relief claimed

T inherited land in June 1988 at a probate value of £290,000. Under a compulsory purchase order, a part of the land is acquired for highway improvements. Compensation of £32,000 and a further £10,000 for severance, neither sum including any amount in respect of loss of profits, is agreed on 14 May 2006. The value of the remaining land is £900,000. Prior to the compulsory purchase, the value of all the land had been £950,000. The indexation factor for the period June 1988 to April 1998 is 0.525.

	£
Total consideration for disposal (£32,000 + £10,000)	42,000
Deduct Allowable cost $\dfrac{42,000}{42,000 + 900,000} \times £290,000$	12,930
Unindexed gain	29,070
Indexation allowance £12,930 × 0.525	6,788
Chargeable gain 2006/07 (subject to TAPER RELIEF (228))	£22,282

(ii) Rollover relief claimed under *TCGA 1992, s 243*

Total consideration for disposal is £42,000, less than 5% of the value of the estate before the disposal (£950,000). T may therefore claim that the consideration be deducted from the allowable cost of the estate.

Revised allowable cost (£290,000 − £42,000)	£248,000

No chargeable gain then arises in 2006/07.

Notes

(*a*)   An indexation adjustment in respect of the amount deducted will be required on a subsequent disposal of the estate. [*TCGA 1992, s 53(3), s 57*]. For an example of the computation, see 206.3(E) CAPITAL SUMS DERIVED FROM ASSETS.

(*b*)   HMRC additionally regard consideration of £3,000 or less as 'small', whether or not it would pass the 5% test illustrated here. (Revenue Tax Bulletin February 1997, p 397).

215.3 **LEASES**

(A) Short leases which are not initially wasting assets [*TCGA 1992, Sch 8 para 1*]
On 31 August 2001, N purchased the remaining term of a lease of commercial premises for £55,000. The lease was subject to a 25-year sub-lease granted on 1 July 1979 at a fixed rental of £1,000 a year. The market rental was estimated at £15,000 a year. The term of the lease held by N is 60 years from 1 April 1977. The value of the lease in 2004, when the sub-lease expired, was estimated at 31 August 2001 as being £70,000. Immediately upon expiry of the sub-lease, N has refurbishment work done at a cost of £50,000, of which £40,000 qualifies as enhancement expenditure. On 31 March 2007, N sells the lease for £130,000.

Term of lease at date of expiry of sub-lease	32 years 9 months
Relevant percentage $89.354 + \frac{9}{12} \times (90.280 - 89.354)$	90.049%
Term of lease at date of assignment	30 years
Relevant percentage	87.330%

	£	£
Disposal consideration		130,000
Deduct Allowable cost	55,000	
Enhancement costs	40,000	
	95,000	
Less Wasted		
$\dfrac{90.049 - 87.330}{90.049} \times 95,000$	2,868	
		92,132
Chargeable gain 2006/07 (subject to TAPER RELIEF (228))		£37,868

Note
(*a*)   The head-lease becomes a wasting asset on the expiry of the sub-lease. [*TCGA 1992, Sch 8 para 1(2)*].

(B) Grant of long lease [*TCGA 1992, s 42, Sch 8 para 2*]

In 1981, K acquired a long lease by assignment for £24,000. At the time he acquired it, the lease had an unexpired term of 83 years. On 10 April 2006, he granted a 55-year sub-lease for a premium of £110,000 and a peppercorn rent. The value of the reversion plus the capitalised value of the rents is £10,000. The value of the lease at 31 March 1982 was estimated at £54,000. The indexation factor for the period March 1982 to April 1998 is 1.047.

	£	£
Disposal consideration	110,000	110,000
Cost £24,000 × $\dfrac{110,000}{110,000 + 10,000}$	22,000	
Market value 31.3.82		
£54,000 × $\dfrac{110,000}{110,000 + 10,000}$		49,500
Unindexed gain	88,000	60,500
Indexation allowance £49,500 × 1.047	51,827	51,827
Gain after indexation	£36,173	£8,673
Chargeable gain 2006/07 (subject to TAPER RELIEF (228))		£8,673

215.3 Land

(C) Grant of short lease [*ICTA 1988, s 34; TCGA 1992, Sch 8 paras 2, 5; ITTOIA 2005, ss 277–281, Sch 1 para 451*]

L is the owner of a freehold factory which he leases for a term of 25 years commencing in December 2006. The cost of the factory was £100,000 in April 1996. The lease is granted for a premium of £30,000 and an annual rent. The reversion to the lease plus the capitalised value of the rents amount to £120,000. The indexation factor for April 1996 to April 1998 is 0.066.

	£	£
Amount chargeable to income tax		
Amount of premium		30,000
Deduct Excluded $\dfrac{25-1}{50} \times £30,000$		14,400
		———
Amount chargeable to income tax		£15,600
Chargeable gain		
Premium received	30,000	
Deduct Charged to income tax	15,600	
	———	
		14,400
Allowable cost $\dfrac{14,400}{30,000 + 120,000} \times £100,000$		9,600
		———
Unindexed gain		4,800
Indexation allowance £9,600 × 0.066		634
		———
Chargeable gain 2006/07 (subject to TAPER RELIEF (228))		£4,166

Notes

(*a*) A short lease is one the duration of which, at the time of grant, does not exceed 50 years.

(*b*) The amount chargeable to income tax is not deducted from the amount of premium appearing in the denominator of the CGT apportionment fraction.

(D) Disposal by assignment of short lease: without enhancement expenditure [*TCGA 1992, Sch 8 para 1*]

X buys a lease for £200,000 on 1 October 2002. The lease commenced on 1 June 1993 for a term of 60 years. X assigns the lease for £300,000 at the end of March 2007.

Term of lease unexpired at date of acquisition	50 years 8 months
Relevant percentage	100%

Term of lease unexpired at date of assignment	46 years 2 months
Relevant percentage $98.490 + \frac{2}{12} \times (98.902 - 98.490)$	98.559%

	£	£
Disposal consideration		300,000
Allowable cost	200,000	
Deduct Wasted $\dfrac{100 - 98.559}{100} \times £200,000$	2,882	
		197,118
Chargeable gain 2006/07 (subject to TAPER RELIEF (228))		£102,882

(E) Disposal by assignment of short lease held at 31 March 1982 [*TCGA 1992, s 35, Sch 8 para 1*]

A buys a lease for £100,000 on 1 March 1982. The lease commenced on 31 March 1972 for a term of 60 years. Its value at 31 March 1982 was estimated at £104,000. On 31 March 2007, A assigns the lease for £240,000. The indexation factor for the period March 1982 to April 1998 is 1.047.

(i) The computation without re-basing to 1982 is as follows

Term of lease unexpired at date of acquisition (1.3.82)	50 years 1 month
Relevant percentage	100%

Term of lease unexpired at date of assignment	25 years 0 months
Relevant percentage	81.1%

215.3 Land

	£	£
Disposal consideration		240,000
Cost	100,000	
Deduct Wasted $\dfrac{100-81.1}{100} \times £100,000$	18,900	81,100
Unindexed gain		158,900
Indexation allowance (see (ii) below)		88,308
Gain after indexation		£70,592

(ii) The computation with re-basing to 1982 is as follows

Term of lease unexpired at deemed date of acquisition (31.3.82)	50 years	
Relevant percentage	100%	
Term of lease unexpired at date of assignment	25 years	
Relevant percentage	81.1%	

	£	£
Disposal consideration		240,000
Market value 31.3.82	104,000	
Deduct Wasted $\dfrac{100-81.1}{100} \times £104,000$	19,656	84,344
Unindexed gain		155,656
Indexation allowance £84,344 × 1.047		88,308
Gain after indexation		£67,348

Chargeable gain 2006/07 (subject to TAPER RELIEF (228))	£67,348

Notes

(a)   A is deemed, under *TCGA 1992, s 35*, to have disposed of and immediately re-acquired the lease on 31 March 1982 at its market value at that date.

(b)   Both calculations produce a gain with the re-basing calculation producing the smaller gain. Therefore, re-basing applies. [*TCGA 1992, s 35(2)(3)(a)*].

(c)   Indexation is based, in both calculations, on the assumption that the asset was sold and re-acquired at market value on 31 March 1982 since this gives a greater allowance than if based on original cost as reduced by the wasting asset provisions. [*TCGA 1992, s 55(1)(2)*].

(F) Disposal by assignment of short lease: with enhancement expenditure [*TCGA 1992, Sch 8 para 1*]

D Ltd acquires the lease of office premises for £100,000 on 1 July 1998. On 1 January 2000, the company contracts for complete refurbishment of the premises at a total cost of £180,000, of which £120,000 can be regarded as capital enhancement expenditure. The work is done at the beginning of January 2000, and the money is payable in equal tranches in March 2000 and May 2000. The lease is for a term of 50 years commencing 1 April 1991. On 1 January 2007, the lease is assigned to a new lessee for £450,000.

Indexation factors (assumed)	July 1998 to January 2007	0.250
	March 2000 to January 2007	0.180
	May 2000 to January 2007	0.170

Term of lease unexpired at date of acquisition	42 years 9 months
Relevant percentage $96.593 + \frac{9}{12} \times (97.107 - 96.593)$	96.978%

Term of lease unexpired at date of expenditure incurred (January 2000 — see note (*a*))	41 years 3 months
Relevant percentage $96.041 + \frac{3}{12} \times (96.593 - 96.041)$	96.179%

Term of lease unexpired at date of assignment	34 years 3 months
Relevant percentage $91.156 + \frac{3}{12} \times (91.981 - 91.156)$	91.362%

	£	£	£
Disposal consideration			450,000
Cost of acquisition	100,000		
Deduct Wasted			
$\dfrac{96.978 - 91.362}{96.978} \times 100,000$	5,791	94,209	
Enhancement expenditure	120,000		
Deduct Wasted			
$\dfrac{96.179 - 91.362}{96.179} \times 120,000$	6,010	113,990	208,199
Unindexed gain			241,801
Indexation allowance			
Cost of lease £94,209 × 0.250		23,552	
Enhancement costs			
March 2000 £56,995 × 0.180		10,259	
May 2000 £56,995 × 0.170		9,689	
			43,500
Chargeable gain			£198,301

Note

(*a*) The wasting provisions apply to enhancement expenditure by reference to the time when it is first reflected in the nature of the lease. The indexation provisions apply by reference to the date the expenditure became due and payable. [*TCGA 1992, s 54(4)(b), Sch 8 para 1(4)(b)*].

(G) Disposal of short lease where premium partly relieved under *ITTOIA 2005, ss 60–67* or *ICTA 1988, s 87*

Butcher acquired a 36-year lease of shop premises from Baker on 1 July 1999 at a premium of £33,000. Butcher prepares trading accounts to 30 June each year. On 1 July 2006, when the unexpired term of the lease is 29 years and property values have risen sharply in the locality, he assigns the lease for £66,000. He makes no other chargeable disposals in 2006/07.

The annual trading deduction under *ITTOIA 2005, ss 60–67* (*formerly ICTA 1988, s 87*) is computed as follows

	£
Premium on 36-year lease	33,000
Deduct $(36 - 1) \times 2\% \times £33,000$	23,100
Premium chargeable on Baker	£9,900

In addition to actual rent payable under the lease, Butcher is entitled to a deduction in computing trading profits in respect of the part of the premium chargeable on Baker, accruing on a day-to-day basis for up to 36 years, of

$$\frac{£9,900}{36} = £275 \text{ p.a.}$$

In his seven accounting years to 30 June 2006, Butcher has thus received a total deduction of $(£275 \times 7) =$ £1,925

The chargeable gain on disposal of the lease in July 2006 is computed as below.

Term of lease unexpired at date of acquisition	36 years
Relevant percentage	92.761%
Term of lease unexpired at date of disposal	29 years
Relevant percentage	86.226%

	£	£
Disposal consideration		66,000
Cost of acquisition	33,000	
Deduct Income tax relief given (see above)	1,925	(note (*a*))
	31,075	
Deduct Wasted $\dfrac{92.761 - 86.226}{92.761} \times £31,075$	2,189	28,886
Pre-tapered gain		37,114
Deduct Business asset taper relief for 7 years $(£37,114 \times 75\%)$		27,836
Chargeable gain		9,278
Deduct Annual exemption		8,800
Taxable gains 2006/07		£478

Notes

(*a*)   The allowable expenditure for CGT is reduced, by virtue of *TCGA 1992, s 39* (exclusion of double relief), by the amount on which income tax relief has been given. This reduction is made *before* the wasting asset reduction required by *TCGA 1992, Sch 8 para 1(4)* (HMRC Capital Gains Manual CG 71201).

(*b*) For further examples on the *income tax* treatment of lease premiums, see (C) above, (H) and (J) below, and IT 21.4 PROPERTY INCOME.

(H) Sub-lease granted out of short lease: premium not less than potential premium
[*TCGA 1992, Sch 8 paras 4, 5*]

On 1 November 2004, S purchased a lease of shop premises then having 50 years to run for a premium of £100,000 and an annual rental of £40,000. After occupying the premises for the purposes of his own business, S granted a sub-lease to N Ltd. The sub-lease was for a term of 21 years commencing on 1 August 2006, for a premium of £50,000 and an annual rental of £30,000. It is agreed that, had the rent under the sub-lease been £40,000, the premium obtainable would have been £20,000.

Term of lease at date granted	50 years
Relevant percentage	100%
Term of lease at date sub-lease granted	48 years 3 months
Relevant percentage $99.289 + \frac{3}{12} \times (99.657 - 99.289)$	99.381%
Term of lease at date sub-lease expires	27 years 3 months
Relevant percentage $83.816 + \frac{3}{12} \times (85.053 - 83.816)$	84.125%

	£
Premium chargeable to income tax on S	
Amount of premium	50,000
Deduct $\dfrac{21-1}{50} \times £50,000$	20,000
Amount chargeable	£30,000
Chargeable gain	
Disposal consideration	50,000
Allowable expenditure	
$£100,000 \times \dfrac{99.381 - 84.125}{100}$	15,256
Chargeable gain	34,744
Deduct Amount chargeable to income tax	30,000
Net chargeable gain 2006/07 (subject to TAPER RELIEF (228))	£4,744

Note

(*a*) If the amount chargeable to income tax had exceeded the chargeable gain, the net gain would have been nil. The deduction cannot create or increase a loss. [*TCGA 1992, Sch 8 para 5(2)*].

(J) Sub-lease granted out of short lease: premium less than potential premium
[TCGA 1992, Sch 8 paras 4, 5; ITTOIA 2005, Sch 1 para 451(2)]
C bought a lease of a house on 1 May 2002, when the unexpired term was 49 years. The cost of the lease was £20,000, and the ground rent payable is £500 p.a. C then let the house on a monthly tenancy until 30 November 2006 when he granted a 10-year lease for a premium of £5,000 and an annual rent of £8,000. Had the rent under the sub-lease been £500 a year, the premium obtainable would have been £40,000. C does not at any time occupy the house as a private residence.

Term of lease at date of acquisition	49 years
Relevant percentage	99.657%
Term of lease when sub-lease granted	44 years 5 months
Relevant percentage $97.595 + \frac{5}{12} \times (98.059 - 97.595)$	97.788%
Term of lease when sub-lease expires	34 years 5 months
Relevant percentage $91.156 + \frac{5}{12} \times (91.981 - 91.156)$	91.500%

Amount chargeable to income tax	£
Amount of premium	5,000
Deduct Exclusion $\dfrac{10-1}{50} \times £5,000$	900
Chargeable to income tax	£4,100

Chargeable gain

Disposal consideration	5,000
Deduct Allowable expenditure	
$£20,000 \times \dfrac{97.788 - 91.500}{99.657} \times \dfrac{5,000}{40,000}$	158
Gain	4,842
Deduct Amount chargeable to income tax	4,100
Net chargeable gain 2006/07 (subject to TAPER RELIEF (228))	£742

Note

(a)   If the amount chargeable to income tax had exceeded the chargeable gain, the net gain would have been nil. The deduction cannot create or increase a loss. *[TCGA 1992, Sch 8 para 5(2)]*.

216   Losses

Cross-references. See IT 13.2 LOSSES for the set-off of trading losses against chargeable gains made by individuals. See 201.2 ANNUAL RATES AND EXEMPTIONS for the interaction between losses and the annual exemption. See also 228.1(B) TAPER RELIEF.

216.1 GENERAL

On 30 April 2006 Q sells for £40,000 a part of the land which he owns. The market value of the remaining estate is £160,000. Q bought the land for £250,000 in March 1996.

	£
Disposal consideration	40,000
Allowable cost $\dfrac{40,000}{40,000 + 160,000} \times £250,000$	50,000
Allowable loss	£10,000

Note

(a)   Indexation allowance cannot increase or create a loss for CGT purposes. [*TCGA 1992, s 53; FA 1994, s 93(1)–(3)*].

216.2 Losses

216.2 PERSONAL LOSSES SET AGAINST ATTRIBUTED SETTLEMENT GAINS

[*TCGA 1992, ss 2(4)–(8), 77; FA 2002, s 51, Sch 11 paras 2, 3, 7, 8*].

In May 2000, R created a UK–resident settlement in which he retained the reversionary interest. It is accepted that *TCGA 1992, s 77* applies to the settlement such that any chargeable gains accruing to the trustees are chargeable on R as settlor (see also 225.2 SETTLEMENTS). In June 2006, the trustees realised a pre-tapered gain of £17,418 on a disposal of quoted securities, a non-business asset for taper relief purposes which they had held since creation of the settlement. They made no other disposal in the year. R, meanwhile, made two disposals in 2006/07 on which he realised a chargeable gain of £4,000 (attracting potential 10% taper relief) and an allowable loss of £9,000. Neither the trustees nor R have any losses brought forward from earlier years. R has taxable income in excess of the basic rate limit.

R's CGT position for 2006/07 is as follows.

	£
Personal gains	4,000
Deduct Personal losses (part) (note (*b*))	4,000
	Nil
Attributed gains (note (*c*))	17,418
Deduct Personal losses (balance) (£9,000 – £4,000)	5,000
	12,418
Deduct Taper relief £12,418 @ 20% (note (*c*))	2,484
	9,934
Deduct Annual exempt amount	8,800
Taxable gains 2006/07	£1,134
CGT payable by R at 40% (recoverable from trustees)	£453.60
Personal losses carried forward	Nil

Notes

(*a*) For 2003/04 onwards, personal losses are deductible without election from *TCGA 1992, s 77* gains. An election under *FA 2002, Sch 11 para 8* to deduct personal losses from such gains is available for any one or more of the years 2000/01, 2001/02 and 2002/03 and must be made no later than 31 January 2005. [*FA 2002, Sch 11 para 8*].

(*b*) Personal losses must be set against personal gains for any particular tax year in priority to attributed gains treated as accruing to the person in that year.

(*c*) Where personal losses are set against an attributed gain, the gain is initially attributed without regard to taper relief. After offsetting the losses, the net attributed gain is then tapered by reference to the period the asset was held by the trustees and its status (business or non-business asset) in their hands.

(*d*) Similar rules apply in the case of gains attributed under *TCGA 1992, s 86* (offshore settlements with settlor interest).

216.3 LOSSES ON SHARES IN UNLISTED TRADING COMPANIES [*ICTA 1988, ss 574–576; FA 2000, s 63(2)(3), Sch 16 para 3(3)*]

P subscribed for 3,000 £1 ordinary shares at par in W Ltd, a qualifying trading company, in June 1988. In September 1995, P acquired a further 2,200 shares at £3 per share from another shareholder. In December 2006, P sold 3,900 shares at 40p per share.

Indexation factors	June 1988 to September 1995	0.413
	September 1995 to April 1998	0.080

Procedure

Firstly, establish the *'section 104* holding' pool.

	Shares	Qualifying expenditure £	Indexed pool £
June 1988 subscription	3,000	3,000	3,000
Indexation to September 1995			
£3,000 × 0.413			1,239
September 1995 acquisition	2,200	6,600	6,600
	5,200	9,600	10,839
Indexed rise: September 1995 to April 1998			
£10,839 × 0.080			867
	5,200	9,600	11,706
December 2006 disposal	(3,900)	(7,200)	(8,780)
Pool carried forward	1,300	£2,400	£2,926

Step 1. Calculate the CGT loss in the normal way, as follows

	£
Disposal consideration 3,900 × £0.40	1,560
Allowable cost $\dfrac{3,900}{5,200}$ × £9,600	7,200
Allowable loss	£5,640

Step 2. Applying a LIFO basis, identify the qualifying shares (1,700) and the non-qualifying shares (2,200) comprised in the disposal.

Step 3. Calculate the proportion of the loss attributable to the qualifying shares.

Loss referable to 1,700 qualifying shares $\dfrac{1,700}{3,900}$ × £5,640   £2,458

Step 4. Compare the loss in Step 3 with the actual cost of the qualifying shares, *viz.*

Cost of 1,700 qualifying shares $\dfrac{1,700}{3,000}$ × £3,000   £1,700

The loss available against income is restricted to £1,700 (being lower than £2,458).

The loss not relieved against income remains an allowable loss for CGT purposes.

£5,640 − £1,700 =   £3,940

216.3 Losses

Notes

(*a*)   Steps 1 to 4 illustrated in this example are those identified by the HMRC Venture Capital Schemes Manual at VCM 47150.

(*b*)   For shares issued after 5 April 1998 (not illustrated above), a company is a qualifying trading company for the purposes of this relief only if it would be a qualifying company for the purposes of the Enterprise Investment Scheme (EIS), although it is not a condition that the company issued the shares under the EIS or that any EIS income tax relief has been, or could have been, claimed in respect of them. [*ICTA 1988, s 576(4)–(4B); FA 2001, Sch 15 para 38*].

(*c*)   For further examples on this topic, see IT 13.5 LOSSES and CT 118.4 LOSSES.

216.4 **DEFERRED UNASCERTAINABLE CONSIDERATION: ELECTION TO TREAT LOSS AS ARISING IN EARLIER YEAR** [*TCGA 1992, ss 279A–279D; FA 2003, s 162*]

Tanya owns 2,000 £1 ordinary shares in Be Good Ltd, for which she subscribed at par in January 1993. The shares qualify as business assets for taper relief purposes. On 31 March 2001, she and the other shareholders in Be Good Ltd sold their shares to another company for £10 per share plus a further unquantified cash amount calculated by means of a formula relating to the future profits of Be Good Ltd. The value in March 2001 of the deferred consideration was estimated at £5.10 per share. Tanya makes no other disposals of chargeable assets in 2000/01. On 30 April 2006, Tanya receives a further £3.60 per share under the sale agreement. The indexation factor for the period January 1993 to April 1998 is 0.179.

Without an election under *TCGA 1992, s 279A*, Tanya's capital gains position is as follows.

2000/01

	£	£
Disposal proceeds	20,000	
Value of rights	10,200	30,200
Cost of acquisition		2,000
Unindexed gain		28,200
Indexation allowance £2,000 × 0.179		358
Pre-tapered gain		27,842
Taper relief £27,842 @ 50%		13,921
Chargeable gain 2000/01		£13,921

2006/07

Disposal of rights to deferred consideration		
Proceeds 2,000 × £3.60		7,200
Deemed cost of acquiring rights		10,200
Allowable loss 2006/07		£3,000

If Tanya makes an election under *TCGA 1992, s 279A* by 31 January 2009 the 2006/07 loss is treated as arising in 2000/01 and can be set off against the gain of that year as follows.

2000/01

	£
Pre-tapered gain as above	27,842
Less Allowable loss	3,000
	24,842
Taper relief £24,842 @ 50%	12,421
Chargeable gain 2000/01	£12,421

Notes

(a) Where a person within the charge to capital gains tax makes a disposal on or after 10 April 2003 of a right to 'future unascertainable consideration' (as defined) acquired as consideration for the disposal of another asset, and a loss accrues, he may, subject to conditions, make an election for the loss to be treated as arising in the year in which that other asset was disposed of. Where the right was acquired as consideration for two or more disposals in different tax years (referred to as '*eligible years*'), the loss is utilised in the earliest year first. [*TCGA 1992, s 279A; FA 2003, s 162(1)(3)*].

(*b*)   To the extent that the loss cannot be utilised in the earliest eligible year it may be carried forward for set-off against gains of later years. In the case of tax years falling between that year and the year of the loss, any remaining part of the loss can only be deducted if the year concerned is an eligible year. [*TCGA 1992, s 279C; FA 2003, s 162(1)*].

(*c*)   The election is irrevocable and must be made by notice in writing to HMRC on or before the first anniversary of 31 January following the year of the loss. The notice must specify the amount of the relevant loss, the right disposed of, the tax year of the right's disposal, and, if different, the year of the loss, the tax year in which the right was acquired, the original asset or assets on disposal of which the right was acquired, the eligible year in which the loss is to be treated as accruing, and the amount to be deducted from gains of that year. [*TCGA 1992, s 279D; FA 2003, s 162(1)*].

217   Married Persons and Civil Partners

Cross-reference. See 228.3 TAPER RELIEF.

217.1 TRANSFERS BETWEEN SPOUSES OR CIVIL PARTNERS AND RATES OF TAX
[*TCGA 1992, ss 4, 58; SI 2005 No 3229, Reg 107*]

(A) No transfer between spouses or civil partners
Paul and Heidi are a married couple with total income of £32,800 and £38,800 respectively for 2006/07. On 4 April 2007, Heidi sells a painting which she had acquired in June 1994 at a cost of £5,000. Net sale proceeds amount to £23,000 and the indexation factor for the period June 1994 to April 1998 is 0.124. Neither spouse disposed of any other chargeable assets during 2006/07.

Chargeable gain — Heidi

	£
Net proceeds	23,000
Cost	5,000
Unindexed gain	18,000
Indexation allowance £5,000 × 0.124	620
Pre-tapered gain	17,380
Taper relief @ 35%	6,083
	11,297
Annual exemption	8,800
Taxable gain	£2,497
Total income	38,800
Personal allowance	5,035
Taxable income	£33,465

Basic rate limit = £33,300, so gain of £2,497 is all taxed at 40%.

Tax payable £2,497 × 40%	£998.80

(B) Transfer between spouses or civil partners
The facts are as in (A) above except that in January 2007, Heidi gives the painting to Paul who then makes the sale on 4 April 2007.

Chargeable gain — Heidi

	£
Deemed consideration (January 2007)	5,620
Cost	5,000
Unindexed gain carried forward	620

217.1   Married Persons and Civil Partners

	£
Unindexed gain brought forward	620
Indexation allowance (to April 1998) £5,000 × 0.124	620
Chargeable gain	Nil

Chargeable gain — Paul

	£
Net proceeds (4.4.07)	23,000
Cost (January 2007)	5,620
Pre-tapered gain	17,380
Taper relief @ 35% (note (b))	6,083
	11,297
Annual exemption	8,800
Taxable gain	£2,497
Total income	32,800
Personal allowance	5,035
Taxable income	£27,765

Taxable income falls short of the basic rate limit (£33,300) by £5,535, so gain of £2,497 is all taxed at 20%.

Tax payable £2,497 × 20%	£499.40
Tax saving compared with (A) above	£499.40

Notes

(a)   The inter-spouse transfer is deemed to be for such consideration as to ensure that no gain or loss accrues. [*TCGA 1992, s 58*]. Effectively, the consideration is equal to cost plus indexation (to April 1998 see 212.1 INDEXATION). See 212.2(A)(B) INDEXATION for further examples. The principles in 212.2(C)(D) INDEXATION also apply.

(b)   Taper relief is computed by reference to the combined period of ownership after 5 April 1998 (see 228.3 TAPER RELIEF). In this instance, relief is at the non-business asset rate of 35% by reference to a qualifying holding period of nine complete years (including the bonus year for assets acquired before 17 March 1998).

(c)   The fact that transfers of assets between husband and wife or between civil partners are no gain/no loss transfers enables savings to be made by ensuring that disposals are made by a spouse or partner with an unused annual exemption and/or basic rate band.

(d)   A transfer between spouses or civil partners followed by a sale could be attacked by HMRC as an anti-avoidance device. To minimise the risk, there should be a clear time interval between the two transactions and no arrangements made to effect the ultimate sale until after the transfer. The gift should be outright with no strings attached and with no 'arrangement' for eventual proceeds to be passed to the transferor.

(e)   The inter-spouse transfer provisions are extended to transfers between same-sex civil partners from 5 December 2005. [*SI 2005 No 3229, Reg 107*].

217.2 **JOINTLY OWNED ASSETS**

Derek and Raquel are a married couple. Derek had for many years owned an investment property which he purchased for £70,000 in May 1988. On 5 January 1996, he transferred to Raquel a 10% share in the property which was thereafter held in their joint names as tenants in common. At the time of the transfer, a 10% share of the property is worth £10,000 on the open market and a 90% share is worth £90,000. No declaration is made for income tax purposes under *ICTA 1988, s 282B*, with the result that the rental income from the property is treated, by virtue of *ICTA 1988, s 282A* as arising in equal shares. On 29 June 2006, the property is sold for £140,000.

Indexation factors May 1988 to January 1996	0.414
May 1988 to April 1998	0.531
January 1996 to April 1998	0.083

(i)   Inter-spouse transfer

	£
Deemed consideration (January 1996)	9,898
Cost £70,000 × $\dfrac{10,000}{10,000 + 90,000}$ (see note (*c*))	7,000
Unindexed gain	2,898
Indexation allowance £7,000 × 0.414	2,898
Chargeable gain 1995/96	Nil

(ii)   2006/07 disposal

	Derek £	Raquel £
Disposal proceeds	126,000	14,000
Cost: Derek (£70,000 – £7,000)	63,000	
Raquel (see (i) above)		9,898
Unindexed gain	63,000	4,102
Indexation allowance: £63,000 × 0.531	33,453	
£9,898 × 0.083		822
Chargeable gains 2006/07 (subject to TAPER RELIEF (228))	£29,547	£3,280

Notes

(*a*)   Where a joint declaration of unequal beneficial interests is made under *ICTA 1988, s 282B*, it is presumed that the same split applies for capital gains tax purposes. In the absence of a declaration, and regardless of the income tax treatment of income derived from the asset, a gain on an asset held in the joint names of husband and wife is apportioned in accordance with their respective beneficial interests at the time of disposal. (Revenue Press Release 21 November 1990).

(*b*)   See 217.1 above as to how the consideration for the inter-spouse transfer is arrived at.

(*c*)   The allowable expenditure on the inter-spouse transfer is apportioned in accordance with the part disposal rules in *TCGA 1992, s 42* (see 208.2 COMPUTATION OF GAINS AND LOSSES).

218   Mineral Royalties

Cross-reference. See also IT 15.1 MINERAL ROYALTIES.

218.1 **GENERAL** [*ICTA 1988, s 122; TCGA 1992, ss 201–203; ITTOIA 2005, ss 157, 319, 340–343, Sch 1 para 106*]

L Ltd, which prepares accounts to 31 December, is the holder of a lease of land acquired in 1993 for £66,000, when the lease had an unexpired term of 65 years. In January 2001, L Ltd grants a 10-year licence to a mining company to search for and exploit minerals beneath the land. The licence is granted for £60,000 plus a mineral royalty calculated on the basis of the value of any minerals won by the licensee. The market value of the retained land (exclusive of the mineral rights) is then £10,000. L Ltd receives mineral royalties as follows

		£
Year ended	31 December 2001	12,000
	31 December 2002	19,000
	31 December 2003	29,000
	31 December 2004	38,000
	31 December 2005	17,000
	31 December 2006	10,000

On 2 January 2007, L Ltd relinquishes its rights under the lease and receives no consideration from the lessor.

(i) Chargeable gains 2001

		£
(*a*)	Disposal proceeds	60,000
	Allowable cost $\dfrac{60,000}{60,000 + 10,000} \times £66,000$	56,571
	Chargeable gain subject to indexation	£3,429
(*b*)	$\frac{1}{2} \times £12,000$	£6,000

(ii) Chargeable gains 2002 to 2006

		£
2002	$\frac{1}{2} \times £19,000$	9,500
2003	$\frac{1}{2} \times £29,000$	14,500
2004	$\frac{1}{2} \times £38,000$	19,000
2005	$\frac{1}{2} \times £17,000$	8,500
2006	$\frac{1}{2} \times £10,000$	5,000

(iii) Loss 2007

	£
Proceeds of disposal of lease	Nil
Allowable cost £66,000 − £56,571	9,429
Allowable loss	£9,429

(iv) The loss may be set off against the chargeable gains arising on the mineral royalties as follows

	£
2006 (whole)	5,000
2005 (part)	4,429
	£9,429

Note

(*a*)   Under *ICTA 1988, s 122* (*ITTOIA 2005, ss 157, 319* for 2005/06 onwards for income tax purposes only) and *TCGA 1992, s 201*, one half of mineral royalties is taxed as income and one half as a chargeable gain. The gain is deemed to accrue in the year of assessment or company accounting period for which the royalties are receivable and is not capable of being reduced by any expenditure or by indexation allowance.

219   Offshore Settlements

Cross-reference. See also 216.2 LOSSES.

219.1 CHARGE ON BENEFICIARY IN RECEIPT OF CAPITAL PAYMENTS

(A) Charge under *TCGA 1992, s 87*

M, resident and domiciled in the UK, is the sole beneficiary of a discretionary settlement created by his father in 2001 and administered in the Cayman Islands. The trustees are all individuals resident in the Cayman Islands. For 2001/02 to 2006/07 the trustees have chargeable gains and allowable losses, and make capital payments to M, as follows

	Chargeable gains £	Allowable losses £	Capital payments £
2001/02	50,000	60,000	20,000
2002/03	80,000	30,000	50,000
2003/04	105,000	—	—
2004/05	—	—	35,000
2005/06	32,000	7,000	20,000
2006/07	—	—	27,000

2001/02	£	£
Trust gains (£50,000 – £60,000)		—
Capital payment		20,000
Balance of capital payment carried forward		£20,000
Trust losses carried forward		£10,000

2002/03		
Trust gains (£80,000 – £30,000 – £10,000)		£40,000
Capital payment	50,000	
Brought forward	20,000	£70,000
Chargeable gains assessable on M		£40,000
Capital payment carried forward (£70,000 – £40,000)		£30,000

2003/04		
Trust gains		£105,000
Capital payment brought forward		£30,000
Chargeable gains assessable on M		£30,000
Trust gains carried forward (£105,000 – £30,000)		£75,000

2004/05	£
Trust gains	—
Trust gains brought forward	75,000
	£75,000
Capital payment	£35,000
Chargeable gains assessable on M	£35,000
Trust gains carried forward (£75,000 − £35,000)	£40,000
2005/06	£
Trust gains (£32,000 − £7,000)	25,000
Trust gains brought forward	40,000
	£65,000
Capital payment	£20,000
Chargeable gains assessable on M	£20,000
Trust gains carried forward (£65,000 − £20,000)	£45,000
2006/07	£
Trust gains	—
Trust gains brought forward	45,000
	£45,000
Capital payment	£27,000
Chargeable gains assessable on M	£27,000
Trust gains carried forward	£18,000

Notes

(a) *TCGA 1992, s 87* applies to a settlement for a tax year if the trustees are neither resident nor ordinarily resident in the UK during any part of the year. [*TCGA 1992, s 87(1); FA 2006, Sch 12 paras 36(1)(2), 41*].

(b) The trust gains for a tax year are treated as chargeable gains accruing in that year to beneficiaries of the settlement who receive capital payments (as defined) from the trustees in that year or have received such payments in any earlier year, such attribution being made in proportion to, but not exceeding, the amounts of capital payments received by them. A capital payment is left out of account for these purposes to the extent that chargeable gains have by reason of the payment been treated as accruing to the recipient in an earlier year. [*TCGA 1992, s 87(4)–(6)*].

(b) The '*trust gains*' for a tax year are the aggregate of

(i)   the amount which would have been chargeable for the current year on the trustees under *TCGA 1992, s 2(2)* (i.e. chargeable gains less current year and brought forward losses), had they been resident and ordinarily resident (for 2006/07 and earlier years, resident or ordinarily resident) in that year; and

(ii) the corresponding amount for any earlier year(s) (1981/82 onwards) which has not yet been attributed under *TCGA 1992, s 87(4)* or *TCGA 1992, s 89(2)* (migrant settlements) to beneficiaries.

[*TCGA 1992, s 87(2); FA 2006, Sch 12 para 34(1)–(3)*].

(*d*) Only beneficiaries domiciled in the UK at some time during the tax year are charged to tax in respect of trust gains attributed to them. [*TCGA 1992, s 87(7)*].

(*e*) See (B) below for the surcharge arising on M's chargeable gains for 2005/06 and 2006/07.

(B) Surcharge on CGT under *TCGA 1992, s 87* [*TCGA 1992, ss 91–93, 97*]
The facts are as in (A) above. For all years M is liable to capital gains tax at 40% on all chargeable gains, but has no gains other than those attributed to him as in (A) above. Surcharge on gains attributed to M under *TCGA 1992, s 87* is calculated as follows.

(i) Qualifying amounts [*TCGA 1992, s 92(1)(2)*]

2001/02		£
Trust's gains		50,000
Deduct Current year losses		60,000
Qualifying amount		—
Losses carried forward		£10,000
2002/03		
Trust's gains		80,000
Deduct Current year losses	30,000	
Losses brought forward	10,000	40,000
Qualifying amount		£40,000
2003/04		
Trust's gains		£105,000
Qualifying amount		£105,000

2004/05
There are no gains accruing to the trust and the qualifying amount is therefore nil.

2005/06	£
Trust's gains	32,000
Deduct Current year losses	7,000
Qualifying amount	£25,000

2006/07
There are no gains accruing to the trust and the qualifying amount is therefore nil.

(ii) Matching capital payments with qualifying amounts [*TCGA 1992, s 92(3)–(6)*]
The capital payment of £20,000 in 2001/02 is matched (on a first in, first out basis) with £20,000 of the qualifying amount for 2002/03.

The £50,000 capital payment in 2002/03 is matched first with the remaining £20,000 of the 2002/03 qualifying amount, and then with £30,000 of the 2003/04 qualifying amount.

The 2004/05 capital payment of £35,000 is matched with £35,000 of the 2003/04 qualifying amount.

The 2005/06 capital payment of £20,000 is matched with £20,000 of the 2003/04 qualifying amount.

The 2006/07 capital payment of £27,000 is matched first with the remaining £20,000 (£105,000 − £30,000 − £35,000 − £20,000) of the 2003/04 qualifying amount and then with £7,000 of the 2005/06 qualifying amount, leaving £18,000 of that amount unmatched.

(iii) Surcharge payable by M [*TCGA 1992, ss 91–93*]
Surcharge is payable where a capital payment is matched with a qualifying amount for a tax year falling at some time before that immediately preceding the one in which the payment is made. In this case, therefore, surcharge is payable in respect of the capital payments in 2005/06 and 2006/07 only, calculated as follows.

	£
2005/06	
CGT payable by M (subject to surcharge)	
(£20,000 − £8,500 annual exemption) × 40%	4,600
Surcharge £4,600 × 10% × 2 years (1.12.04–30.11.06)	920
Total tax payable	£5,520
2006/07	
CGT payable by M (subject to surcharge)	
(£27,000 − £8,800 annual exemption) × 40%	7,280
Surcharge on part of payment (£20,000) matched with 2003/04 qualifying amount:	
(£20,000/£27,000) × £7,280 = £5,392 × 10% × 3 years (1.12.04–30.11.07)	1,618
Total tax payable	£8,898

Notes

(*a*)   The surcharge is 10% per annum for a period beginning on 1 December following the end of the tax year of the qualifying amount concerned and ending on 30 November in the tax year following that in which the capital payment is made but subject to a maximum period of 6 years. [*TCGA 1992, s 91(3)–(5)*].

(*b*)   In arriving, for surcharge purposes, at the CGT payable on the capital payment, that payment (or part) is deemed to form the lowest slice of the taxpayer's total gains (and may be reduced by the annual exemption). HMRC consider that where the payment is matched with qualifying amounts from different tax years, the tax should be apportioned pro rata (and this is the method illustrated above for 2006/07). (HMRC Helpsheet IR 301).

(*c*)   Personal capital losses cannot be set against gains attributed to an individual under *TCGA 1992, s 87*. [*TCGA 1992, s 2(4)(5)*]. See also 201.2(B) ANNUAL RATES AND EXEMPTIONS.

219.1 Offshore Settlements

(C) Charge under *TCGA 1992, s 87* — **further example**
T and M are the only beneficiaries under a Jersey settlement set up by their grandfather. None of the trustees is resident in the UK.

T is resident in the UK but M is neither resident nor ordinarily resident in the UK. Both beneficiaries have a UK domicile. In 2005/06, the trustees sell shares realising a chargeable gain of £102,000. No disposals are made in 2006/07.

The trustees make capital payments of £60,000 to M in 2005/06. In 2006/07 they make capital payments of £60,000 to T and £10,000 to M.

2005/06	£
Trust gains	102,000
Capital payment	60,000
Trust gains carried forward	£42,000

M has chargeable gains of £60,000 but is not subject to CGT.

2006/07	£
Trust gains (brought forward)	42,000
Capital payments (£60,000 + £10,000)	70,000
Balance of capital payments carried forward	£28,000

The chargeable gains are apportioned as follows

		£
T	$\dfrac{60,000}{70,000} \times £42,000$	36,000
M	$\dfrac{10,000}{70,000} \times £42,000$ (not assessable)	6,000
		£42,000

The capital payments carried forward are apportioned as follows

	£
T £60,000 − £36,000	24,000
M £10,000 − £6,000	4,000
	£28,000

(D) Distributions of income and gains [*ICTA 1988, s 740(6); TCGA 1992, ss 87, 97*]
A Liechtenstein foundation was created in 1966 by a UK resident domiciled in Scotland. None of the trustees is resident in the UK and the trust administration is carried on in Switzerland. The foundation has the following income and chargeable gains for 2004/05 to 2006/07.

	Income £	Chargeable gains £
2004/05	15,000	5,000
2005/06	24,000	12,000
2006/07	30,000	3,000

L, who is resident and domiciled in the UK and is the only current beneficiary, receives payments of £28,000 in 2004/05 and £50,000 in 2006/07.

	Total £	Income £	Chargeable gains £
2004/05			
Total income/gains	20,000	15,000	5,000
Payment	28,000	15,000	5,000
Balance	Nil	Nil	Nil
Balance of payment c/f	£8,000		
2005/06			
Total income/gains	36,000	24,000	12,000
Payment (balance b/f)	8,000	8,000	—
Balance c/f	£28,000	£16,000	£12,000
2006/07			
Total income/gains	33,000	30,000	3,000
Brought forward	28,000	16,000	12,000
	61,000	46,000	15,000
Payment	50,000	46,000	4,000
Balance c/f against future payments	£11,000	—	£11,000

Summary of taxable amounts

	Income tax £	Chargeable gains £
2004/05	15,000	5,000
2005/06	8,000	—
2006/07	46,000	4,000

220   Overseas Matters

220.1 **COMPANY MIGRATION** [*TCGA 1992, ss 185, 187*]

Z Ltd is a company incorporated in Ruritania, but regarded as resident in the UK by virtue of its being managed and controlled in the UK. It is the 75% subsidiary of Y plc, a UK resident company. On 1 October 2006, the management and control of Z Ltd is transferred to Ruritania and it thus ceases to be UK resident, although it continues to trade in the UK, on a much reduced basis, via a UK permanent establishment.

Details of the company's chargeable assets immediately before 1 October 2006 were as follows.

	Market value	Capital gain after indexation (where applicable) if all assets sold
	£	£
Factory in UK	480,000	230,000
Warehouse in UK	300,000	180,000
Factory in Ruritania	350,000	200,000
Warehouse in Ruritania	190,000	100,000
UK quoted investments	110,000	80,000
Foreign trade investments	100,000	Loss (60,000)

The UK warehouse continues to be used in the UK trade. The UK factory does not, and is later sold. On 1 June 2007, the Ruritanian warehouse is sold for the equivalent of £210,000. On 1 October 2008, Y plc sells its shareholding in Z Ltd.

Prior to becoming non-UK resident, Z Ltd had unrelieved capital losses brought forward of £40,000.

The corporation tax consequences assuming no election under *TCGA 1992, s 187* are as follows

Chargeable gain accruing to Z Ltd on 1.10.06

	£
Factory (UK)	230,000
Factory (Ruritania)	200,000
Warehouse (Ruritania)	100,000
UK quoted investments	80,000
Foreign trade investments	(60,000)
	550,000
Losses brought forward	40,000
Net gain chargeable to corporation tax	£510,000

The later sale of the UK factory does not attract corporation tax as the company is non-resident and the factory has not, since the deemed reacquisition immediately before 1 October 2006, been used in a trade carried on in the UK through a permanent establishment. Similarly, the sale of the overseas warehouse, and of any other overseas assets, is outside the scope of corporation tax on chargeable gains. Any subsequent disposal of the UK warehouse *will* be within the charge to corporation tax, having been omitted from the deemed disposal on 1 October 2006, due to its being used in a trade carried on in the UK through a permanent establishment. On disposal, the gain will be computed by reference to original cost, or 31.3.82 value if appropriate, rather than to market value immediately before 1 October 2006 — see also note (*d*).

Y plc will realise a capital gain (or loss) on the sale of its shareholding in Z Ltd on 1 October 2008.

The corporation tax consequences if an election is made under *TCGA 1992, s 187* are as follows

Chargeable gain accruing to Z Ltd on 1.10.06

	£
Factory (UK)	230,000
UK quoted investments	80,000
	310,000
Losses brought forward	40,000
Net gain liable to corporation tax	£270,000

Postponed gain on foreign assets

	£
Factory (Ruritania)	200,000
Warehouse (Ruritania)	100,000
	300,000
Foreign trade investments	(60,000)
	£240,000

On 1 June 2007, a proportion of the postponed gain becomes chargeable as a result of the sale, within six years of Z Ltd's becoming non-resident, of one of the assets in respect of which the postponed gain accrued. The gain chargeable to corporation tax as at 1 June 2007 on Y plc is

$$\frac{100{,}000 \text{ (postponed gain on warehouse)}}{300{,}000 \text{ (aggregate of postponed gains)}} \times £240{,}000 = £80{,}000$$

On 1 October 2008, in addition to any gain or loss arising on the sale of the shares, Y plc will be chargeable to corporation tax on the remainder of the postponed gain, i.e. on £160,000 (£240,000 – £80,000), by virtue of Z Ltd having ceased to be its 75% subsidiary as a result of the sale of shares.

The position as regards the UK warehouse is the same as if no election had been made.

Notes

(*a*)   The provisions of *TCGA 1992, s 185* apply where a company ceases to be resident in the UK. All companies incorporated in the UK are regarded as UK resident. As such a company cannot therefore cease to be resident, *section 185* can apply only to companies incorporated abroad which are UK resident. See also HMRC Statement of Practice SP 1/90 as regards company residence generally.

(*b*)   If, with an election, Z Ltd's unrelieved capital losses had exceeded its chargeable gains arising on 1 October 2006, the excess could have been allowed against postponed gains at the time when they become chargeable on Y plc, subject to the two companies making a joint election to that effect under *TCGA 1992, s 187(5)*.

220.2   Overseas Matters

(c)   *FA 1988, ss 130–132* contain management provisions designed to secure payment of all outstanding tax liabilities on a company becoming non-UK resident. See also HMRC Statement of Practice SP 2/90.

(d)   If the UK warehouse ceases to be a chargeable asset by virtue of Z Ltd's ceasing to carry on a trade in the UK through a permanent establishment, there will be a deemed disposal at market value at that time, under *TCGA 1992, s 25*. See 220.2 below.

220.2   **NON-RESIDENTS CARRYING ON TRADE, ETC. THROUGH UK BRANCH OR AGENCY** [*TCGA 1992, ss 10, 25*]

X, who is not resident and not ordinarily resident in the UK, practises abroad as a tax consultant and also practises in the UK through a London branch, preparing accounts to 5 April. The assets of the UK branch include premises bought in 1988 for £60,000 and a computer acquired in March 2003 for £20,000. On 31 January 2007, the computer ceases to be used in the UK branch and is immediately shipped abroad, and on 28 February 2007, X closes down the UK branch. He sells the premises in June 2007 for £118,000. Capital allowances claimed on the computer up to and including 2005/06 were £13,250 and short-life asset treatment had been claimed.

Relevant market values of the assets are as follows

	£
Computer, at 31 January 2007	11,000
Premises, at 14 March 1989	65,000
at 28 February 2007	110,000
Indexation factor March 1989 to April 1998	0.448

The UK capital gains tax consequences are as follows

	£	£
Computer		
Market value 31.1.07		11,000
Deduct Cost	20,000	
Less capital allowances claimed (note (*f*))	9,000	11,000
Chargeable gain		Nil

	£
Premises	
Market value 28.2.07	110,000
Deduct Market value 14.3.89	65,000
Unindexed gain	45,000
Indexation allowance £65,000 × 0.448	29,120
Chargeable gain	£15,880

Net chargeable gains 2006/07 (subject to TAPER RELIEF (228))	£15,880

Notes

(a) X is within the charge to UK capital gains tax for disposals after 13 March 1989 by virtue of his carrying on a profession in the UK through a branch or agency. Previously, the charge applied only to non-residents carrying on a *trade* in this manner. X is deemed to have disposed of (with no capital gains tax consequences) and reacquired immediately before 14 March 1989 all chargeable assets used in the UK branch at market value, so that any subsequent CGT charge will be by reference only to post-13 March 1989 gains. [*FA 1989, s 126(3)–(5); TCGA 1992, s 10(5)*].

(b) There is a deemed disposal, at market value, of the computer on 31 January 2007 as a result of its ceasing to be a chargeable asset by virtue of its becoming situated outside the UK. [*TCGA 1992, s 25(1)*].

(c) There is a deemed disposal, at market value, of the premises on 28 February 2007 as a result of the asset ceasing to be a chargeable asset by virtue of X's ceasing to carry on a trade, profession or vocation in the UK through a branch or agency. [*TCGA 1992, s 25(3)(8)*]. See also note (g) below.

(d) There are no UK CGT consequences on the actual disposal of the premises in June 2007.

(e) X is entitled to the £8,800 annual exemption against UK gains, regardless of his residence status.

(f) Where a chargeable asset has qualified for capital allowances and a loss accrues on its disposal, the allowable expenditure is restricted, under *TCGA 1992, s 41*, by the net allowances given, which in this example amount to £9,000 (first-year and writing-down allowances £13,250 less balancing charge £4,250 arising on the asset's ceasing to be used in the trade).

(g) *TCGA 1992, s 25(3)* (see note (c) above) does not apply, on a claim under *TCGA 1992, s 172*, in relation to an asset where a non-UK resident company transfers its trade (carried on through a UK permanent establishment) to a UK resident company in the same group. The asset is deemed to be transferred at no gain/no loss. For disposals after 31 March 2000, this applies automatically under *TCGA 1992, s 171* without the need for any claim. [*TCGA 1992, s 172; FA 2000, Sch 29 para 3*].

220.3 **TRANSFER OF ASSETS TO NON-RESIDENT COMPANY** [*TCGA 1992, s 140*]

Q Ltd, a UK resident company, carries on business in a foreign country through a branch there. In September 2000, it is decreed that all enterprises in that country be carried on by locally resident companies. Q Ltd forms a wholly-owned non-UK resident subsidiary R and transfers all the assets of the branch to R wholly in consideration for the issue of shares. The assets transferred include the following

	Value	Chargeable gains
	£	£
Goodwill	100,000	95,000
Freehold land	200,000	120,000
Plant (items worth more than £6,000)	50,000	20,000
Other assets	150,000	—
	£500,000	£235,000

In March 2002, there is a compulsory acquisition of 50% of the share capital of R for £300,000 (market value). The value of the whole shareholding immediately before disposal is £750,000. The value of Q Ltd's remaining 50% holding is £300,000.

In June 2006, R is forced to sell its freehold land to the government.

Q Ltd's capital gains position is as follows

2000
The gain of £235,000 is deferred. The allowable cost of the shares in R is £500,000.

2002

		£
Consideration on disposal		300,000

Add
Proportion of deferred gain $£235,000 \times \dfrac{300,000}{750,000}$ — 94,000

394,000

Deduct
Cost of shares sold $£500,000 \times \dfrac{300,000}{300,000 + 300,000}$ — 250,000

Gain subject to indexation — £144,000

2006
Proportion of deferred gain chargeable — £

Gain arising $\dfrac{120,000}{235,000} \times £235,000$ — £120,000

Balance of gain still held over
(£235,000 − £94,000 − £120,000) — £21,000

Notes
(a) The 2006 gain arises under *section 140(5)*. If the sale of freehold land had taken place more than six years after the original transfer of assets, no part of the deferred gain would have become chargeable as a result.

(b) The 2002 gain arises under *section 140(4)*. In this case, there is no time limit as in (a) above.

(c) The 2002 gain is subject to indexation allowance on £250,000 from September 2000 to March 2002.

221   Partnerships

221.1 **ASSETS** [*TCGA 1992, s 59*]

G, H and I trade in partnership. They share capital in the ratio 5:4:3. Land occupied by the firm is sold on 15 April 2006 for £240,000, having been acquired for £60,000 in 1981. The agreed market value of the land at 31 March 1982 is £54,000. G has elected under *TCGA 1992, s 35(5)* for his personal assets held on 31 March 1982 to be treated as disposed of and re-acquired at their market value on that date. G has personal gains in 2006/07 of £2,500, H has losses of £1,000 and I made no disposals of personal assets. None of the partners has any capital losses brought forward from earlier years. The partnership land was a business asset throughout for taper relief purposes but the personal assets sold by G and H were non-business assets (held in G's case for less than three years). The indexation factor for the period March 1982 to April 1998 (note (*b*)) is 1.047.

The gains of G, H and I, without re-basing to 1982, are as follows

	G ($\frac{5}{12}$)	H ($\frac{4}{12}$)	I ($\frac{3}{12}$)
	£	£	£
Disposal consideration	100,000	80,000	60,000
Cost	25,000	20,000	15,000
Unindexed gain	75,000	60,000	45,000
Indexation allowance Cost × 1.047	26,176	20,940	15,706
Gain after indexation	£48,824	£39,060	£29,294

The gains of G, H and I, with re-basing to 1982, are as follows

	G ($\frac{5}{12}$)	H ($\frac{4}{12}$)	I ($\frac{3}{12}$)
	£	£	£
Disposal consideration	100,000	80,000	60,000
Market value 31.3.82	22,500	18,000	13,500
Unindexed gain	77,500	62,000	46,500
Indexation allowance (as above)	26,176	20,940	15,706
Gain after indexation	£51,324	£41,060	£30,794

Summary

	G	H	I
	£	£	£
Share of partnership gain	48,824	39,060	29,294
Personal gains/(losses)	2,500	(1,000)	—
Chargeable gain	51,324	38,060	29,294
Taper relief @ 75% on £48,824/£38,060/£29,294	36,618	28,545	21,971
	14,706	9,515	7,323
Annual exemption	8,800	8,800	7,323
Taxable gain 2006/07	£5,906	£715	Nil

Notes

(*a*)   An individual partner's election under *TCGA 1992, s 35(5)* in respect of his personal assets does not extend to his share of partnership assets and *vice versa*, this being by virtue of *TCGA 1992, s 35(7)*. (See HMRC Statement of Practice SP 4/92, para 10(i).)

(b)   Other than for the purposes of corporation tax on chargeable gains, indexation allowance is frozen at its April 1998 level. See 212 INDEXATION.

221.2 **CHANGES IN SHARING RATIOS**

J and K have traded in partnership for many years, sharing capital and income equally. The acquisition costs and 31 March 1982 values of the chargeable assets of the firm are as follows

	Cost	31.3.82 value
	£	£
Premises	60,000	150,000
Goodwill	10,000	50,000

The assets have not been revalued in the firm's balance sheet. On 1 June 2006, J and K admit L to the partnership, and the sharing ratio is J 35%, K 45% and L 20%. The indexation factor for March 1982 to April 1998 is 1.047.

J and K are regarded as disposing of part of their interest in the firm's assets to L as follows

	£	£
J		
Premises		
Deemed consideration		
£60,000 × (50% − 35%)	9,000	
Add indexation allowance (see below)	23,558	
Total deemed consideration	32,558	
Allowable cost	9,000	
Unindexed gain	23,558	
Indexation allowance (50% − 35%) × £150,000 × 1.047	23,558	—
Goodwill		
Deemed consideration		
£10,000 × (50% − 35%)	1,500	
Add indexation allowance (see below)	7,853	
Total deemed consideration	9,353	
Allowable cost	1,500	
Unindexed gain	7,853	
Indexation allowance (50% − 35%) × £50,000 × 1.047	7,853	—
Chargeable gain/allowable loss		Nil

108

K

Premises

Deemed consideration	
£60,000 × (50% − 45%)	3,000
Add indexation allowance (see below)	7,853
Total deemed consideration	10,853
Allowable cost	3,000
Unindexed gain	7,853
Indexation allowance (50% − 45%) × £150,000 × 1.047	7,853 —

Goodwill

Deemed consideration	
£10,000 × (50% − 45%)	500
Add indexation allowance (see below)	2,618
Total deemed consideration	3,118
Allowable cost	500
Unindexed gain	2,618
Indexation allowance (50% − 45%) × £50,000 × 1.047	2,618 —

Chargeable gain/allowable loss	Nil

The allowable costs (inclusive, in L's case, of indexation allowance to April 1998) of the three partners are now

		Freehold land £	Goodwill £
J		21,000	3,500
K		27,000	4,500
L	(note (*c*))	43,411	12,471

Notes

(*a*)   The treatment illustrated above is taken from HMRC Statement of Practice SP D12 (17.1.75), para 4 as extended by SP 1/89. Each partner's disposal consideration is equal to his share of current balance sheet value of the asset concerned plus, for disposals after 5 April 1988, indexation allowance to April 1998, and each disposal treated as producing no gain and no loss.

(*b*)   As the deemed disposals are no gain/no loss disposals, re-basing to 1982 does not apply. The incoming partner, having acquired his share in the assets by means of a no gain/no loss disposal after 31 March 1982 is regarded as having held the asset at that date for the purposes of re-basing on a subsequent disposal. (HMRC Statement of Practice SP 1/89).

(*c*)   L's allowable costs comprise 20% of original cost, plus indexation allowance to April 1998 based on 20% of 31 March 1982 value.

(*d*)   See 212.2(A)(C) INDEXATION for an example of the indexation adjustments required on a subsequent disposal other than a no gain/no loss disposal.

221.3   Partnerships

221.3 ACCOUNTING ADJUSTMENTS

A, B and C trade in partnership. They share income and capital profits equally. The firm's only chargeable asset is its premises which cost £51,000 in 1989. C decides to retire. The remaining partners agree to share profits equally. Before C retires (in May 2006), the premises are written up to market value in the accounts, agreed at £81,000. C does not receive any payment directly from the other partners on his retirement.

The capital gains tax consequences are

On retiring, C is regarded as having disposed of his interest in the firm's premises for a consideration equal to his share of the then book value.

		£
Disposal consideration	$\frac{1}{3} \times$ £81,000	27,000
Acquisition cost	$\frac{1}{3} \times$ £51,000	17,000
Gain subject to indexation to April 1998 and taper relief		£10,000

A and B will each be treated as acquiring a $\frac{1}{6}$ ($\frac{1}{2} \times \frac{1}{3}$) share in the premises, at a cost equal to one half of C's disposal consideration. Their acquisition costs are then

		A	B
		£	£
Cost of original share	$\frac{1}{3} \times$ £51,000	17,000	17,000
Cost of new share	$\frac{1}{2} \times$ £27,000	13,500	13,500
Total		£30,500	£30,500

221.4 CONSIDERATION OUTSIDE ACCOUNTS

D, E and F are partners in a firm of accountants who share all profits in the ratio 7:7:6. G is admitted as a partner in May 2006 and pays the other partners £10,000 for goodwill. The new partnership shares are D $\frac{3}{10}$, E $\frac{3}{10}$, F $\frac{1}{4}$ and G $\frac{3}{20}$. The book value of goodwill is £18,000, its cost on acquisition of the practice from the predecessor in 1990.

The partners are treated as having disposed of shares in goodwill as follows

D	£	£
$\frac{7}{20} - \frac{3}{10} = \frac{1}{20}$		
Disposal consideration		
Notional $\frac{1}{20} \times £18,000$	900	
Actual $\frac{7}{20} \times £10,000$	3,500	
		4,400
Allowable cost $\frac{1}{20} \times £18,000$		900
Unindexed gain		£3,500
E		
$\frac{7}{20} - \frac{3}{10} = \frac{1}{20}$		
Disposal consideration (as for D)		4,400
Allowable cost (as for D)		900
Unindexed gain		£3,500
F		
$\frac{6}{20} - \frac{1}{4} = \frac{1}{20}$		
Disposal consideration		
Notional $\frac{1}{20} \times £18,000$	900	
Actual $\frac{6}{20} \times £10,000$	3,000	
		3,900
Allowable cost		900
Unindexed gain		£3,000

G's allowable cost of his share of goodwill is therefore		
Actual consideration paid		10,000
Notional consideration paid $\frac{3}{20} \times £18,000$		2,700
		£12,700

Note

(a) In practice, the above calculations must be adjusted for indexation allowance to April 1998 which is added to the notional consideration and deducted from the unindexed gain — see 221.2 above and HMRC Statement of Practice SP 1/89. Any chargeable gains remaining after indexation are reduced by TAPER RELIEF (228).

221.5 Partnerships

221.5 SHARES ACQUIRED IN STAGES

Q is a partner in a legal practice. The partnership's only chargeable asset is a freehold house used as a surgery. The cost of the house to the partnership was £3,600 in 1962 and it was revalued in the partnership accounts to £50,000 in 1990. Q was admitted to the partnership in June 1964 with a share of $\frac{1}{6}$ of all profits. As a result of partnership changes, Q's profit share altered as follows

1970 $\frac{1}{5}$
1981 $\frac{1}{4}$
2006 $\frac{3}{10}$

For capital gains tax, Q's allowable cost of his share of the freehold house is calculated as follows

		£	
1964	$\frac{1}{6} \times £3,600$		£600
1970	$(\frac{1}{5} - \frac{1}{6}) \times £3,600$	120	
1981	$(\frac{1}{4} - \frac{1}{5}) \times £3,600$	180	
2006	$(\frac{3}{10} - \frac{1}{4}) \times £50,000$	2,500	£2,800

Notes

(a) The pre- and post-6.4.65 costs are not pooled.

(b) On Q's acquisition of an increased share of the property in 2006 (subsequent to the revaluation in 1990), any partner with a reduced share will be treated as having made a disposal and thus a gain or loss. The re-basing rules of *TCGA 1992, s 35* will apply to the disposal (subject to the usual comparison with the gain or loss without re-basing).

221.6 **PARTNERSHIP ASSETS DISTRIBUTED IN KIND**

R, S and T are partners sharing all profits in the ratio 4:3:3. Farmland owned by the firm is transferred in November 2006 to T for future use by him as a market gardening enterprise separate from the partnership business. No payment is made by T to the other partners but a reduction is made in T's future share of income profits. The book value of the farmland is £5,000, its cost in 1991, but the present market value is £15,000.

		£
R		
Deemed disposal consideration	$\frac{4}{10} \times £15,000$	6,000
Allowable cost	$\frac{4}{10} \times £5,000$	2,000
Gain (subject to indexation allowance to April 1998 and TAPER RELIEF (228))		£4,000
S		
Deemed disposal consideration	$\frac{3}{10} \times £15,000$	4,500
Allowable cost	$\frac{3}{10} \times £5,000$	1,500
Gain (subject to indexation allowance to April 1998 and TAPER RELIEF (228))		£3,000
T		
Partnership share	$\frac{3}{10} \times £5,000$	1,500
Market value of R's share		6,000
Market value of S's share		4,500
Allowable cost of land for future disposal		£12,000

222　Private Residences

222.1 PERIODS OF OWNERSHIP QUALIFYING FOR EXEMPTION AND LET PROPERTY EXEMPTION [*TCGA 1992, ss 222, 223*]

(A)

P sold a house on 1 July 2006 realising an otherwise chargeable gain (before taper relief) of £54,000. The house was purchased on 1 February 1980 and was occupied as a residence until 30 June 1987 when P moved to another residence, letting the house as residential accommodation. He did not re-occupy the house prior to its sale.

	£
Gain on sale	54,000
Deduct Exempt amount under main residence rules	
$\dfrac{5\text{y }3\text{m} + 3\text{y}}{24\text{y }3\text{m}} \times £54,000$	18,371
	35,629
Deduct Let property exemption	18,371
Net chargeable gain (subject to TAPER RELIEF (228))	£17,258

Notes

(*a*)　The final three years of ownership are always included in the exempt period of ownership. [*TCGA 1992, s 223(1)*].

(*b*)　The period of ownership for the exemption calculation does not include any period before 31 March 1982. This applies regardless of whether the gain has been calculated by reference to cost or to 31 March 1982 value under the re-basing rules. [*TCGA 1992, s 223(7)*].

(*c*)　The gain attributable to the letting (£35,629) is exempt to the extent that it does not exceed the lesser of £40,000 and the gain otherwise exempt (£18,371 in this example). [*TCGA 1992, s 223(4)*].

(B)

Q bought a house on 1 August 1981 for £40,000 and used it as his main residence. On 10 February 1982, he was sent by his employer to manage the Melbourne branch of the firm and continued to work in Australia until 4 August 1987, the whole of his duties being performed outside the UK. The house was let as residential accommodation during that period. Q took up residence in the house once again following his return to the UK, but on 30 September 1994 moved to Switzerland for health reasons. On this occasion, the property was not let. He returned to the UK in August 1997, but did not reside in the house at any time prior to its being sold on 31 December 2006 for £252,350. The house had a market value of £50,000 at 31 March 1982 and the indexation factor for the period March 1982 to April 1998 (note (*f*)) is 1.047.

Computation of gain before applying exemptions

	£	£
Disposal consideration	252,350	252,350
Cost	40,000	
Market value 31.3.82		50,000
Unindexed gain	212,350	202,350
Indexation allowance £50,000 × 1.047	52,350	52,350
Gain after indexation	£160,000	£150,000
Gain before applying exemptions		£150,000

The gain is reduced by the main residence exemptions as follows

Period of ownership (excluding period before 31.3.82)		24y 9m
Exempt periods since 31.3.82:		
31.3.82 – 30.9.94	12y 6m	
1.1.04 – 31.12.06 (last three years)	3y 0m	15y 6m

		£
		150,000

Gain as above
Deduct Exempt amount under main residence rules

$$\frac{15\text{y } 6\text{m}}{24\text{y } 9\text{m}} \times £150,000$$

		93,939
		56,061

Deduct Let property exemption:

Period of letting 31.3.82 – 4.8.87	5y 4m	

Gain attributable to letting $\dfrac{5\text{y } 4\text{m}}{24\text{y } 9\text{m}} \times £150,000 =$ £32,323

Exemption (note (*e*))		32,323
Net chargeable gain 2006/07 (subject to taper relief)		23,738

Notes

(*a*) Periods of ownership before 31 March 1982 are excluded in applying the main residence exemptions. This is the case even if re-basing to 1982 does not apply. [*TCGA 1992, s 223(7)*].

(*b*) The period spent in Australia (regardless of its length but excluding that part of it before 31 March 1982) counts as a period of residence, as Q worked in an employment all the duties of which were performed outside the UK and used the house as his main residence at some time before and after this period of absence. [*TCGA 1992, s 223(3)(b)*].

(*c*) The period spent in Switzerland would have been exempt, having not exceeded three years, but the exemption is lost as Q did not occupy the property as a main residence at any time after this period. [*TCGA 1992, s 223(3)(a)*].

(*d*) The last three years of ownership are always exempt providing the property has been used as the owner's only or main residence at some time during the period of ownership, and for this purpose, 'period of ownership' is not restricted to the period after 30 March 1982. [*TCGA 1992, ss 222, 223(1)*].

(e)   The let property exemption is the lesser of the gain attributable to the period of letting (£32,323), the gain otherwise exempt (£93,939) and £40,000. It cannot create a loss. It is available only if the property is let as residential accommodation. [*TCGA 1992, s 223(4)*].

(f)   Other than for the purposes of corporation tax on chargeable gains, indexation allowance is frozen at its April 1998 level. Therefore, the indexation factor for April 1998 is used in respect of disposals in a later month (and expenditure incurred in April 1998 or later does not attract indexation allowance at all). See 212 INDEXATION.

222.2   ELECTION FOR MAIN RESIDENCE [*TCGA 1992, s 222(5)*]

S purchased the long lease of a London flat on 1 June 1997. He occupied the flat as his sole residence until 31 July 1999 when he acquired a property in Shropshire. Both properties were thereafter occupied as residences by S until the lease of the London flat was sold on 28 February 2007, realising an otherwise chargeable gain of £75,000.

The possibilities open to S are

(i) Election for London flat to be treated as main residence throughout

Exempt gain   £75,000

(ii) Election for Shropshire property to be treated as main residence from 31.7.99 onwards

Exempt gain £75,000 $\times \dfrac{2y\ 2m + 3y}{9y\ 9m}$ £39,744

(iii) Election for London flat to be treated as main residence up to 28 February 2004, with election for the Shropshire property to be so treated thereafter

Exempt gain £75,000 $\times \dfrac{6y\ 9m + 3y}{9y\ 9m}$ £75,000

Note

(a)   The elections in (iii) are the most favourable, provided they could have been made by 31 July 2001 in respect of the London flat, and by 28 February 2006 in respect of the Shropshire property. Note that the last three years' ownership of the London flat is an exempt period in any case. The advantage of (iii) over (i) is that the period of ownership 1 March 2004 to 28 February 2007 of the Shropshire property will be treated as a period of residence as regards any future disposal of that property. HMRC practice is that the *initial* election (which can be varied) must be made within two years of acquisition of the second property, and this was upheld in *Griffin v Craig-Harvey Ch D 1993, 66 TC 396, [1994] STC 54*.

222.3 PART BUSINESS USE [*TCGA 1992, s 224(1) (2)*]

T purchased a freehold property for £50,000 on 30 April 1987. It consists of living room, two bedrooms, kitchen, bathroom and spare room. T and his family occupy the house as their main residence. T runs a small accountancy practice for which he rented office accommodation until October 1990 when a rent review made it less economical. From 1 November 1990, he uses the spare room at home exclusively for business. On 1 February 2007, T sells the property for £190,000. T makes one other disposal in 2006/07, realising a gain, after taper relief, of £4,000. The indexation factor for the period April 1987 to April 1998 is 0.597.

T's chargeable gain on disposal of the property may be computed as follows

	£	£
Net proceeds		190,000
Cost		50,000
Unindexed gain		140,000
Indexation allowance £50,000 × 0.597		29,850
Gain after indexation		110,150
Deduct Private residence exemption		

$$£110,150 \times \frac{3y\ 6m\ +\ 3y}{19y\ 9m} \times 100\% \text{ (note }(b)\text{)} \qquad 36,252$$

$$£110,150 \times \frac{13y\ 3m}{19y\ 9m} \times \frac{5\ \text{rooms}}{6\ \text{rooms}} \text{ (notes }(a)(b)\text{)} \qquad 61,582 \qquad 97,834$$

		£
Gain attributable to business use		12,316
Deduct Taper relief (see below)		5,132
Chargeable gain		7,184
Gain on other disposal		4,000
Total chargeable gains		11,184
Deduct Annual exemption		8,800
Taxable gain 2006/07		£2,384

Computation of taper relief (note (c))

Relevant period of ownership	6.4.98–1.2.07
Business use throughout that period (1 room out of 6)	1/6
Proportion of gain qualifying for business asset taper (£12,316 × 1/6)	£2,053
Proportion qualifying for non-business asset taper (£12,316 × 5/6)	£10,263

The qualifying holding period consists of eight whole years but with a one-year addition (the bonus year) in respect of the non-business asset proportion as the property was acquired before 17 March 1998.

	£
Business asset taper relief £2,053 @ 75%	1,540
Non-business asset taper relief £10,263 @ 35%	3,592
Total taper relief	£5,132

222.3   Private Residences

Notes

(*a*)   Only the gain on the part of the house used *exclusively* for business is excluded from qualifying for the private residence exemption. [*TCGA 1992, s 224(1)*]. In this example, it is considered reasonable to compute that gain by apportioning the whole gain by reference to the use to which rooms are put. In a case where the value of the business part of mixed property is disproportionately higher than that of the private part, it would be more appropriate to apportion the proceeds by reference to respective values and compute two separate gains, only one of which will attract the exemption (see HMRC Capital Gains Manual CG 64670–64674).

(*b*)   Where there has been change of use of part of a house, private residence relief is adjusted as is 'just and reasonable'. [*TCGA 1992, s 224(2)*]. Simple time apportionment of the gain over the period of ownership is considered to give the most sensible result in this example. Note that because the business part of the house has *at some time* in the period of ownership been used as part of the main residence, the last three years of ownership are included in the 100% exempt period of ownership (see HMRC Capital Gains Manual CG 64765, 64988, 64989).

(*c*)   Although the pre-tapered gain can be said to be entirely attributable to the business part of the property, *TCGA 1992, Sch A1 para 9* requires the gain to be apportioned for taper relief purposes (i.e. between business and non-business asset) by reference to the use to which the entire asset (i.e. the whole house) has been put during its period of ownership since 6 April 1998. This arguably inequitable interpretation has apparently been confirmed by HMRC (see *Taxation 12 December 2002 p 271*).

(*d*)   If T were to purchase a replacement property which again has a part used exclusively for the business he could choose to roll over the pre-tapered gain against the cost of that part of the new property under the rules illustrated in 224 ROLLOVER RELIEF — REPLACEMENT OF BUSINESS ASSETS.

222.4 **HOLD-OVER RELIEF OBTAINED ON EARLIER DISPOSAL** [*TCGA 1992, ss 226A, 226B: FA 2004, s 117, Sch 22 paras 6–8*]

On 1 January 2003, Isobel gives a house which she has not occupied as a private residence to the trustees of a discretionary trust of which she is the settlor. She claims hold-over relief under *TCGA 1992, s 260* in respect of the disposal (see 211.1 HOLD-OVER RELIEFS) and the chargeable gain of £80,000 is held over. The trustees allow Isobel's daughter, Lyra, to occupy the house, under the terms of the settlement, as her main residence from 1 January 2003 to 31 December 2004. The house is then sold by the trustees on 20 January 2005 for £300,000. The market value of the house at 1 January 2003 is agreed to be £200,000. The trust is not a settlor-interested settlement for the purposes of *TCGA 1992, ss 169B–169G*.

The trustees' chargeable gain on disposal of the house is as follows.

	£	£
Disposal consideration		300,000
Cost	200,000	
Deduct held-over gain	80,000	120,000
Gain		180,000
Deduct Private residence exemption		
£180,000 × 343/751 (note (*b*))		82,210
Chargeable gain 2004/05		£97,790

Notes

(*a*)   Subject to transitional rules (see (*b*) below), private residence relief under *TCGA 1992, s 223* is not available for disposals by individuals or trustees after 9 December 2003 where, in computing the chargeable gain which would (apart from that relief) accrue on that disposal, the allowable expenditure falls to be reduced to any extent in consequence, directly or indirectly, of a claim or claims under *TCGA 1992, s 260* (see 211.1 HOLD-OVER RELIEFS) in respect of one or more earlier disposals (whether or not made to the person making the later disposal). [*TCGA 1992, s 226A: FA 2004, s 117, Sch 22 para 6*].

(*b*)   Where the earlier disposal to which the *TCGA 1992, s 260* claim relates, or, if more than one, each of the earlier disposals, is made before 10 December 2003, total exemption (under *TCGA 1992, s 223(1)*) is excluded, but fractional exemption (under *TCGA 1992, s 223(2)*) can be obtained. In calculating the fractional exemption, the dwelling-house (or part thereof) in question is taken not to have been the individual's only or main residence at any time after 9 December 2003, and the period of ownership after that date is taken not to form part of the last 36 months of the period of ownership. In this case, the house was occupied as Lyra's main residence for 343 days before 10 December 2003 (i.e. 1 January 2003 to 9 December 2003, and the trustees' total period of ownership was 751 days (1 January 2003 to 20 January 2005).

(*c*)   No taper relief is available to the trustees on disposal of the house, as it is a non-business asset owned for less than three years. Isobel's period of ownership of the house does not count as part of the trustees' period of ownership.

223 Qualifying Corporate Bonds

[TCGA 1992, ss 115–117]

223.1 **DEFINITION** *[TCGA 1992, s 117]*

B has the following transactions in 5% unsecured loan stock issued in 1983 by F Ltd.

		£
11.11.83	Purchase £2,000	1,800
10.7.89	Gift from wife £1,000 (original cost £800)	—
30.9.97	Purchase £2,000	2,100
5.6.06	Sale £4,000	(3,300)

Apart from the gift on 10.7.89, all acquisitions were arm's length purchases. B's wife acquired her £1,000 holding on 11.11.83. Indexation allowance of £266 arose on the transfer from wife to husband.

For the purposes of the accrued income scheme, the sale is without accrued interest and the rebate amount is £20. The stock is a corporate bond as defined by *TCGA 1992, s 117(1)* and a 'relevant security' as defined by *TCGA 1992, s 108(1)*.

Under the rules for matching relevant securities in *TCGA 1992, s 106A*, the stock disposed of is identified with acquisitions as follows.

(i) Identify £2,000 with purchase on 30.9.97 (LIFO)

	£
Disposal consideration £3,300 × $\frac{2,000}{4,000}$	1,650
Add rebate amount £20 × $\frac{2,000}{4,000}$	10
	1,660
Allowable cost	2,100
Loss	£440

The loss is *not* allowable as the £2,000 stock purchased on 30.9.97 is a qualifying corporate bond (note (*a*)). *[TCGA 1992, s 115]*.

(ii) Identify £1,000 with acquisition on 10.7.89

	£
Disposal consideration £3,300 × $\frac{1,000}{4,000}$	825
Add rebate amount £20 × $\frac{1,000}{4,000}$	5
	830
Allowable cost (including indexation to 10.7.89)	1,066
Allowable loss	£236

The loss is allowable as the stock acquired on 10.7.89 is not a qualifying corporate bond (note (*b*)).

(iii) Identify £1,000 with purchase on 11.11.83

	£
Disposal consideration £3,300 × $\frac{1,000}{4,000}$	825
Add rebate amount £20 × $\frac{1,000}{4,000}$	5
	830
Allowable cost £1,800 × $\frac{1,000}{2,000}$	900
Allowable loss	£70

The loss is allowable as the stock acquired on 11.11.83 is not a qualifying corporate bond (note (c)).

Notes

(a)   The acquisition on 30.9.97 is a qualifying corporate bond as it was acquired after 13 March 1984 otherwise than as a result of an excluded disposal. [*TCGA 1992, s 117(7)(b)*].

(b)   The acquisition on 10.7.89 was the result of an excluded disposal, being a no gain/ no loss transfer between spouses where the first spouse had acquired the stock before 14 March 1984. It is therefore not a qualifying corporate bond. [*TCGA 1992, s 117(7)(b)(8)*].

(c)   Securities acquired before 14 March 1984 cannot be qualifying corporate bonds in the hands of the person who so acquired them.

(d)   See IT 2 ACCRUED INCOME SCHEME for the income tax effects of the accrued income scheme.

223.2 **REORGANISATION OF SHARE CAPITAL** [*TCGA 1992, s 116*]

D holds 5,000 £1 ordinary shares in H Ltd. He acquired the shares in April 1992 by subscription at par. On 1 August 1995, he accepted an offer for the shares from J plc. The terms of the offer were one 25p ordinary share of J plc and £10 J plc 10% unsecured loan stock (a qualifying corporate bond) for each H Ltd ordinary share. Both the shares and the loan stock are listed on the Stock Exchange. In December 2006, D sells £20,000 loan stock at its quoted price of £105 per cent.

The value of J plc ordinary shares at 1 August 1995 was £3.52 per share and the loan stock was £99.20 per cent. The indexation factor for April 1992 to August 1995 is 0.080.

The cost of the H Ltd shares must be apportioned between the J plc ordinary shares and loan stock.

	£
Value of J plc shares	
5,000 × £3.52	17,600
Value of J plc loan stock	
£50,000 × 99.2%	49,600
	£67,200

Allowable cost of J plc shares

$$\frac{17,600}{67,200} \times £5,000 \qquad\qquad £1,310$$

Allowable cost of J plc loan stock

$$\frac{49,600}{67,200} \times £5,000 \qquad\qquad £3,690$$

223.2 Qualifying Corporate Bonds

Chargeable gain on H Ltd shares attributable to J plc loan stock to date of exchange

	£
Deemed disposal consideration	49,600
Allowable cost	3,690
Unindexed gain	45,910
Indexation allowance £3,690 × 0.080	295
Deferred chargeable gain	£45,615

Deferred chargeable gain accruing on disposal of loan stock in December 2006

Loan stock sold (nominal)	£20,000
Total holding of loan stock before disposal (nominal)	£50,000

Deferred chargeable gain accruing in 2006/07

$$\frac{20,000}{50,000} \times £45,615 \qquad £18,246$$

Notes

(a)   The gain on the sale of J plc loan stock is exempt (as the stock is a qualifying corporate bond) except for that part which relates to the gain on the previous holding of H Ltd shares. [*TCGA 1992, s 115, s 116(10)*]. There will also be income tax consequences under the accrued income scheme (see IT 2 ACCRUED INCOME SCHEME).

(b)   For taper relief purposes, the deferred gain is deemed to arise in August 1995 (and not in December 2006). [*TCGA 1992, Sch A1 para 16; FA 1998, s 121(2)(4), Sch 20*]. Thus, there can be no taper relief due in this example.

(c)   The qualifying corporate bond is treated as acquired at the date of the reorganisation, so even if the original shares had been held at 31 March 1982, re-basing could *not* apply on the subsequent disposal of the loan stock. However, where the original shares were acquired before 31 March 1982, the reorganisation took place before 6 April 1988, and the qualifying corporate bonds are disposed of after 5 April 1988, the deferred chargeable gain is halved. [*TCGA 1992, Sch 4 para 4*].

(d)   The exchange of J plc ordinary shares for H Ltd shares is dealt with under *TCGA 1992, ss 127–130*, and no gain or loss will arise until the J plc shares are disposed of. See 226.4 SHARES AND SECURITIES.

224   Rollover Relief — Replacement of Business Assets

Cross-reference. See also 205.2 ASSETS HELD ON 31 MARCH 1982 for relief under *TCGA 1992, s 36, Sch 4* for certain gains accruing before 31 March 1982.

[*TCGA 1992, ss 152–158*]

224.1 **NATURE OF RELIEF** [*TCGA 1992, s 152*]

(A)

N Ltd carries on a manufacturing business. It makes the following disposals and acquisitions of assets during the company's accounting periods ended 31 December 2004, 31 December 2005 and 31 December 2006.

	Asset	Bought/ (sold) £	Chargeable gains £
1.10.04	Freehold depot	18,000	—
12.12.04	Leasehold warehouse	(50,000)	28,000
19.6.05	Business formerly carried on by another (unrelated) company:		
	Goodwill (note (*c*))	20,000	—
	Freehold factory unit	90,000	—
1.2.06	Land adjacent to main factory, now surplus to requirements	(40,000)	19,000
8.9.06	Industrial mincer (fixed plant)	(30,000)	5,000
1.11.06	Extension to new factory	35,000	—

(i) The gain on the leasehold warehouse may be rolled over against the following

	Cost £		Gain £
Freehold depot	18,000	$\dfrac{18,000}{50,000} \times £28,000$	10,080
Freehold factory (part)	32,000	$\dfrac{32,000}{50,000} \times £28,000$	17,920
	£50,000		£28,000

See note (*b*)

(ii) The gain on the surplus land may then be rolled over as follows

Freehold factory (part)	£40,000	Gain rolled over	£19,000

(iii) The gain on the industrial mincer may be rolled over as follows

Extension to new factory (part)	£30,000	Gain rolled over	£5,000

224.1 Rollover Relief — Replacement of Business Assets

The position at 31 December 2006 is then as follows

	£
Freehold depot	
Cost	18,000
Deduct gains rolled over	10,080
Allowable cost	£7,920
Freehold factory	
Cost	90,000
Deduct gains rolled over (£17,920 + £19,000)	36,920
Allowable cost	£53,080
Extension to new factory	
Cost	35,000
Deduct gains rolled over	5,000
Allowable cost	£30,000

Notes

(*a*) The expenditure still available to match against disposal proceeds is

Extension to factory (£35,000 − £30,000)   £5,000

The expenditure is available only against disposals up to 31 October 2007.

(*b*) There is no statutory rule prescribing the way in which the gain on an asset must be rolled over against a number of different assets. The taxpayer's allocation of the rolled over gain against the cost of the new assets should be accepted by HMRC, providing specified amounts of consideration are positively earmarked and set against the cost of specified new assets (HMRC Capital Gains Manual, CG60775). In (i) the chargeable gain has been rolled over rateably to the costs of the items, but bringing in only part (i.e. the balance of proceeds) of the cost of the freehold factory.

(*c*) For corporation tax purposes, goodwill acquired from an unrelated party after 31 March 2002 falls within the intangible assets regime at *FA 2002, Sch 29* and is *not* a qualifying asset for chargeable gains rollover relief purposes. [*FA 2002, s 84, Sch 29 paras 132(5), 137*].

(B)

L Ltd carries on a vehicle repair business. In December 2002 it sells a workshop for £90,000 net of costs. The workshop had cost £45,000 inclusive in April 1994. A new workshop is purchased for £144,000 (including incidental costs of acquisition) on 11 January 2003 and sold for £168,000 on 14 January 2007.

Indexation factors	April 1994 to December 2002	0.238
	January 2003 to January 2007 (estimated)	0.110

L Ltd claims rollover of the chargeable gain on the disposal of the workshop.

	£
Allowable cost of original workshop	45,000
Indexation allowance £45,000 × 0.238	10,710
	55,710
Actual disposal consideration	90,000
Chargeable gain rolled over	£34,290
Cost of new workshop	144,000
Deduct Amount rolled over	34,290
Deemed allowable cost	£109,710
Disposal consideration, replacement workshop	168,000
Allowable cost	109,710
Unindexed gain	58,290
Indexation allowance £109,710 × 0.110	12,068
Chargeable gain (January 2007)	£46,222

(C)

The facts are as in (B) above except that the business is carried on by M, an individual. M makes no disposals in 2006/07 other than that of the replacement workshop. The indexation factor for the period April 1994 to April 1998 is 0.128.

	£
Allowable cost of original workshop	45,000
Indexation allowance £45,000 × 0.128	5,760
	50,760
Actual disposal consideration	90,000
Chargeable gain rolled over (note (*a*))	£39,240
Cost of new workshop	144,000
Deduct Amount rolled over	39,240
Deemed allowable cost	£104,760
Disposal consideration, replacement workshop	168,000
Allowable cost	104,760
Gain subject to taper relief	£63,240
Business asset taper relief: £63,240 @ 75% (note (*b*))	47,430
Chargeable gain 2006/07 (note (*b*))	£15,810

224.2   Rollover Relief — Replacement of Business Assets

Notes

(a)   No taper relief is available on a rolled over gain (see Tolley's Capital Gains Tax 2006/07 at 61.17 TAPER RELIEF).

(b)   The qualifying holding period of the replacement workshop for taper relief purposes runs from 11 January 2003 to 14 January 2007, comprising more than two complete years. [*TCGA 1992, s 2A; FA 1998, s 121(1); FA 2000, s 66*]. The period of ownership of the original workshop is not taken into account. Two years is sufficient (for disposals after 5 April 2002) to attract the maximum 75% taper relief on assets that have been business assets throughout the period of ownership.

(c)   Other than for the purposes of corporation tax on chargeable gains, indexation allowance is frozen at its April 1998 level. Therefore, the indexation factor for April 1998 is used in respect of disposals in a later month (and expenditure incurred in April 1998 or later does not attract indexation allowance at all). See 212 INDEXATION.

224.2 PARTIAL RELIEF

(A) Assets only partly replaced [*TCGA 1992, s 153*]

G carries on an accountancy practice. In March 2006, he agrees to acquire the practice of another sole practitioner, who is about to retire. As part of the acquisition, G pays £20,000 for goodwill. In January 2007, G moves to new premises, acquiring the remaining 70 years of a 99-year lease for £50,000. The sale of his former office on 25 February 2007 realises £80,000, and a chargeable gain (after indexation to April 1998) of £59,000 arises. (The former office had been owned since 1992.)

	£	£
Amount of proceeds of disposal of old office		80,000
Costs against which gains can be rolled over		
Goodwill	20,000	
Lease	50,000	
		70,000
Chargeable gain not rolled over		10,000
Business asset taper relief @ 75% (note (*c*))		7,500
Chargeable gain		£2,500
Chargeable gain rolled over (£59,000 − £10,000)		£49,000
Allowable cost of assets (see note (*a*))		
Goodwill	20,000	
Gain rolled over $\dfrac{20,000}{70,000} \times £49,000$	14,000	
		£6,000
Lease	50,000	
Gain rolled over $\dfrac{50,000}{70,000} \times £49,000$	35,000	
		£15,000

Notes

(*a*)   There is no statutory rule prescribing the way in which a gain is to be rolled over against more than one acquisition. See note (*b*) to 224.1(A) above.

(*b*)   It would not have been possible to roll over the gain only against the acquisition of the goodwill. The consideration not reinvested (£60,000) would be more than the gain (£59,000).

(*c*)   The qualifying holding period for taper relief purposes runs from 6 April 1998 to 25 February 2007, comprising eight complete years. [*TCGA 1992, s 2A; FA 1998, s 121(1); FA 2000, s 66*].

(*d*)   A gain does not qualify for taper relief to the extent that it is rolled over (see Tolley's Capital Gains Tax 2006/07 at 61.17 TAPER RELIEF).

(B) Partial business use [*TCGA 1992, s 152(7)*]

N carries on a consultancy business from commercial premises formerly used as a shop. N has owned the property since 1 July 1981, but it was let until 1 March 1993 when N moved in, following the expiry of the lease held by the former tenant. On 1 February 2007, N sells the property for £100,000, moving to a new office with a long lease which he acquires for £60,000 and which is wholly used for his business. The value at 31 March 1982 of the property sold was £40,000 and N has made the global re-basing election under *TCGA 1992, s 35(5)*. The indexation factor for March 1982 to April 1998 is 1.047.

For rollover relief purposes, N is treated as having disposed of two separate assets, one representing his occupation and professional use of the property, the other his ownership of it as an investment. In practice, the proceeds and chargeable gain may be allocated by a simple time apportionment.

Proceeds attributable to business use

Proceeds £100,000 × $\dfrac{13y\ 11m}{24y\ 10m}$ (note (*c*))   £56,040

Chargeable gain attributable to business use

[£100,000 − £40,000 − (£40,000 × 1.047)] = £18,120 × $\dfrac{13y\ 11m}{24y\ 10m}$ £10,154

Notes

(*a*)   The proceeds attributable to business use are less than the cost of the new office, so that the whole of the chargeable gain attributable to business use can be rolled over. The allowable cost of the new office is then £49,846 (£60,000 − £10,154).

(*b*)   The balance of the chargeable gain, £7,986 (£18,120 − £10,154) is not eligible for rollover. It *is* fully eligible for business asset taper relief by reference solely to the use of the property after 5 April 1998 (see 228.2 TAPER RELIEF).

(*c*)   The time apportionment takes into account only the period of ownership after 30 March 1982. [*TCGA 1992, s 152(9)*].

224.3   Rollover Relief — Replacement of Business Assets

224.3 **WASTING ASSETS** [*TCGA 1992, s 154*]

(A) Crystallisation of held-over gain
In March 2002, a father and son partnership carrying on a car dealing trade sold a freehold showroom for £400,000 realising a chargeable gain (after indexation) of £190,000. On 30 June 2002, the firm purchased for £450,000 the remaining term of a lease due to expire on 30 June 2032 and used the premises as a new showroom. The whole of the gain on the old asset was held over under *TCGA 1992, s 154* on the acquisition of the new asset. In consequence of the father's decision to retire from the business and the resulting need to downsize the operation, the firm assigns the lease for £490,000 on 1 July 2006.

The chargeable gains to be apportioned between the two partners for 2006/07 are as follows

	£	£
Proceeds of assignment		490,000
Cost (see note (*a*))	450,000	
Deduct Wasted $\dfrac{87.330 - 82.496}{87.330} \times £450,000$	24,909	425,091
Chargeable gain 2006/07 (see also note (*b*))		£64,909
Held-over gain becoming chargeable under *TCGA 1992, s 154(2)(a)*		£190,000

Notes
(*a*)   The gain of £190,000 is deferred as opposed to being rolled over and does not reduce the cost of the new asset.

(*b*)   Each of the partners will be entitled to taper relief on their share of the gain of £64,909 to the extent that it is not reduced by the offset of capital losses. Taper relief on the deferred gain of £190,000 operates by reference to the date of disposal and period of ownership of the old asset. See 228.4 TAPER RELIEF.

(*c*)   See also 215.3(D)–(G) LAND for further examples on the assignment of short leases.

(B) Rollover of held-over gain

C Ltd, a manufacturing company, sells an item of fixed plant for £30,000 in February 2002. A chargeable gain of £7,200 arises. In 2004, the company buys storage facilities on a 20-year lease for £40,000. In 2006, an extension to the company's freehold factory is completed at a cost of £25,000.

The position is as follows

(i) The company may claim holdover of the £7,200 chargeable gain in 2002, against the cost of the lease.

(ii) In 2006, part of the chargeable gain can be rolled over against the cost of the factory extension, as follows

	£
Expenditure available for rollover	25,000
Maximum capable of rollover	
£7,200 – (£30,000 – £25,000)	2,200
Adjusted base cost of extension	£22,800

Notes

(*a*) The balance of the chargeable gain, £5,000 (£7,200 – £2,200) may continue to be held over against the cost of the lease, either until it crystallises or until further rollover is possible.

(*b*) Had the company not claimed holdover against the cost of the lease, a claim against the cost of the extension in 2006 would not have been possible, as the expenditure was incurred outside the normal three-year time limit.

225   Settlements

Cross-reference. See 219.1 OFFSHORE SETTLEMENTS as regards capital gains of non-resident settlements.

225.1   **ANNUAL EXEMPTIONS AND RATES OF TAX** [*TCGA 1992, ss 3, 4(1AA), Sch 1 paras A1, 2; FA 2004, s 29; FA 2006, Sch 12 paras 28, 38, 44(1)*]

The trustees of the E settlement, created in 1974, realise net chargeable gains and allowable losses, all on disposals of non-business assets for taper relief purposes, as follows

	Chargeable gain/ (allowable loss) £
2002/03	(2,250)
2003/04	3,100
2004/05	4,700
2005/06	3,200
2006/07	11,550

The settlor does not have an interest in the settlement (see note (*b*)).

The trustees' capital gains tax liability is computed as follows

	£
2002/03	
Taxable amount	Nil
Losses carried forward	£2,250
2003/04	
Net chargeable gains	3,100
Losses brought forward	—
Taxable amount (covered by annual exemption of £3,950)	£3,100
CGT	Nil
Losses carried forward	£2,250
2004/05	
Net chargeable gains	4,700
Losses brought forward	600
Taxable amount (covered by annual exemption)	£4,100
CGT	Nil
Losses carried forward (£2,250 − £600)	£1,650
	£
2005/06	
Net chargeable gains	3,200
Losses brought forward	—
Taxable amount (covered by annual exemption of £4,250)	£3,200
CGT	Nil
Losses carried forward	£1,650

2006/07

Net chargeable gains	11,550
Losses brought forward	1,650
Untapered gains	9,900
Deduct Taper relief @ 35% (note (*c*))	3,465
Taxable gains	£6,435
CGT at 40% on £2,035 (6,435 − 4,400)	£814.00
Losses carried forward	Nil

Notes

(*a*) The rate of capital gains tax on gains accruing to the trustees of any settlement, whether it be an interest in possession trust or an accumulation and maintenance trust is equivalent to the income tax 'rate applicable to trusts'. The rate is 40% for 2006/07. [*TCGA 1992, s 4(1AA); ICTA 1988, s 686(1A); FA 2004, s 29*].

(*b*) If the settlor had an interest in the settlement (as defined by *TCGA 1992, s 77(2)–(5)*) at any time during 2006/07, the gain of £6,435 (after deducting losses and taper relief but before deducting the annual exemption) would be chargeable on the settlor and not on the trustees. His own annual exemption of £8,800 may be set against the gain (see also 201.2(B) ANNUAL RATES AND EXEMPTIONS and 216.2 LOSSES). Any tax payable could be recovered from the trustees. See also 225.2 below. [*TCGA 1992, ss 77–79*].

(*c*) It is assumed that the 2006/07 chargeable gains all arose on disposals of assets acquired before 17 March 1998, thus giving a qualifying holding period for taper relief purposes of seven years plus the bonus year for non-business assets so acquired.

(*d*) See *TCGA 1992, Sch 1 para 2(4)–(6)* for the annual exemption available to two or more settlements made by the same settlor after 6 June 1978.

225.2 Settlements

225.2 SETTLEMENT IN WHICH SETTLOR HAS AN INTEREST [*TCGA 1992, ss 77–79; FA 2002, Sch 11 paras 3, 8; FA 2006, Sch 12 paras 3, 13, 31, 33*]

In May 2004 Henry, a UK resident, settled £25,000 on trust to his wife for her life with the remainder to his adult daughter absolutely. The trustees are resident in the UK. For 2005/06, the trustees make disposals on which they incur losses of £300. For 2006/07, they realise gains of £4,000 and losses of £700 (these figures being net of any available taper relief). Henry has personal gains of £8,000 for 2006/07 (again after any available taper relief) with no losses brought forward. Henry's taxable income for 2006/07 is £50,000 and he is thus liable to tax at 40% on capital gains.

Henry's capital gains tax liability for 2006/07 is calculated as follows

	£	£
Personal gains		8,000
Settlement gains	4,000	
Deduct Losses	700	
	3,300	
Deduct Losses b/f	300	3,000
		11,000
Deduct Annual exemption		8,800
Gain liable to CGT		£2,200
CGT payable at 40%		£880.00
CGT recoverable from trustees (note (*a*))		£880.00

Notes

(*a*) For the purposes of recovery from the trustees, the settlement gains are regarded as forming the highest part of the total amount on which Henry is liable to CGT. His personal gains are therefore fully covered by his annual exemption and the whole of the liability relates to the settlement gains; it is thus fully recoverable from the trustees. [*TCGA 1992, s 78*].

(*b*) If either Henry or his wife died during 2006/07, or if they ceased to be married during that year, *TCGA 1992, ss 77–79* would not apply and the settlement gain of £3,300 (before deducting losses brought forward) would be covered by the trustees' annual exemption of £4,400, with losses of £300 carried forward to 2007/08. [*TCGA 1992, s 77(6)*].

(*c*) For the offset of personal capital losses of the settlor against gains attributed to him under the rules illustrated in this example, see 216.2 LOSSES.

225.3 TRUSTS WITH VULNERABLE BENEFICIARY [*FA 2005, ss 23–45, Sch 1; FA 2006, Sch 12 para 48, Sch 13 para 35*]

Harry was born in 1997. In June 2004 both of his parents are killed in a road accident. Neither parent has made a will, so that a statutory trust is established for Harry under the intestacy rules of *Administration of Estates Act 1925, ss 46, 47(1)*. The trustees and Harry's guardian make a vulnerable person election (by 31 January 2008) to take effect on 6 April 2005. On 16 May 2006, the trustees sell an asset, realising a chargeable gain of £20,000. The asset is a non-business asset for taper relief purposes. The trustees (who are resident in the UK throughout) make no other disposals in 2006/07. Harry is resident in the UK throughout the tax year and has no taxable income and no personal chargeable gains.

If the trustees make a claim for special tax treatment under *FA 2005*, *s 24* for 2006/07, Harry's capital gains tax liability is calculated as follows.

	£
Settlement gain	20,000
Deduct Annual exemption	8,800
Gain liable to CGT	£11,200

CGT payable

£		£
2,150 @10%		215.00
9,050 @20%		1,810.00
11,200		£2,025.00

CGT recoverable from trustees	£2,025.00

Notes

(a)   No taper relief is due as the asset is a non-business asset held by the trustees for less than three years.

(b)   Where a claim for special tax treatment is made for a tax year and the vulnerable beneficiary is UK resident during the year, chargeable gains arising to the trustees are taxable on the beneficiary under *TCGA 1992*, *ss 77–79* (see 225.2 above) as if that beneficiary were a settlor and had an interest in the settlement during the year. [*FA 2005*, *s 31*]. The tax payable by the beneficiary is recoverable from the trustees. Effectively, this allows the trustees to make use of the beneficiary's annual exemption and basic rate band, where available.

(c)   If no claim had been made by the trustees for special tax treatment, the trustees' CGT liability would have been £6,240 (£20,000 less annual exemption £4,400 = £15,600 @ 40%).

(d)   A claim for special tax treatment applies to both income tax and capital gains tax. No separate claim can be made in respect of each tax.

(e)   Where the vulnerable beneficiary is not UK resident, more complex rules apply, for which see *FA 2005*, *ss 32, 33, Sch 1*.

225.4 CREATION OF A SETTLEMENT [*TCGA 1992, s 70*]

(A)

In December 2006, C transfers to trustees of a settlement for the benefit of his disabled daughter 10,000 shares in W plc, a quoted company. The value of the gift is £85,000. C bought the shares in 1981 for £20,000 and their value at 31 March 1982 was £35,000. The indexation factor for March 1982 to April 1998 is 1.047.

225.4 Settlements

	£	£
Deemed disposal consideration	85,000	85,000
Cost	20,000	
Market value 31.3.82		35,000
Unindexed gain	65,000	50,000
Indexation allowance £35,000 × 1.047	36,645	36,645
Gain after indexation	£28,355	£13,355
Chargeable gain (subject to TAPER RELIEF (228))		£13,355
Trustees' allowable cost		£85,000

Note

(a) If the transfer had been a chargeable lifetime transfer for inheritance tax purposes, or would be one but for the annual inheritance tax exemption and the settlement is not settlor-interested within *TCGA 1992, ss 169B–169G*, C could have elected under *TCGA 1992, s 260* to roll the gain over against the trustees' base cost of the shares. The trustees do not join in any such election. It is the *untapered* gain that is held over (see Tolley's Capital Gains Tax 2006/07 at 61.16 TAPER RELIEF).

(B)

In late April 2006 H settles farmland on trust for himself for life, with interests in reversion to his children. The land cost £20,000 in 1975 and its agreed values are £60,000 at 31 March 1982 and £125,000 at the date of settlement. H's interest in possession in the settled property is valued at £90,000. The indexation factor from March 1982 to April 1998 is 1.047.

The chargeable gain is computed as follows

	£	£
Deemed disposal proceeds	125,000	125,000
Cost	20,000	
Market value 31.3.82		60,000
Unindexed gain	105,000	65,000
Indexation allowance £60,000 × 1.047	62,820	62,820
Gain after indexation	£42,180	£2,180
Chargeable gain 2006/07 (subject to TAPER RELIEF (228))		£2,180

Notes

(a) The value of H's interest in the settled property is ignored and the transfer is not treated as a part disposal.

(b) For as long as H has an interest in the settlement the provisions of *TCGA 1992, ss 77–79* will apply to any settlement gains, with the effect that they will be chargeable on the settlor and not on the trustees. See 225.2 above.

(c) As the settlement is settlor-interested, H cannot claim hold-over relief under *TCGA 1992, s 260* even though the transfer of the land into settlement is a chargeable lifetime transfer. See note (a) to (A) above.

225.5 **PERSON BECOMING ABSOLUTELY ENTITLED TO SETTLED PROPERTY**
[*TCGA 1992, s 71*]

(A)
M is a beneficiary entitled to an interest in possession in settled property, under a settlement made by her mother. The trustees exercise a power of appointment to advance capital to M, and, in September 2006, transfer to her a house valued at £80,000. The house was acquired by the trustees by gift from the settlor in 2002, when its value was £45,000.

The trustees realise a gain of £35,000 (£80,000 – £45,000) (before any taper relief) on the advancement of capital to M.

Notes
(a)   Taper relief is available, by reference to the trustees' period of ownership after 5 April 1998.

(b)   If, while it was settled property, the house had been occupied by M as her private residence with the permission of the trustees, then all or part of the gain would qualify for the private residence exemption under *TCGA 1992, s 225*.

(B) Transfer of settlement losses [*TCGA 1992, s 71(2)–(2D)*]
F is the sole remaining beneficiary of an accumulation and maintenance settlement established under his late uncle's will and in which he became entitled to an interest in possession upon reaching the age of 18 in 1996. On 18 September 2003, his 25th birthday, he becomes absolutely entitled as against the trustees to the capital of the trust. At that date, the trust capital consists of the following

- cash of £12,000,

- 10,000 shares in ABC Ltd (purchased for £6,000 in May 2002 and currently valued at £11,000), and

- 15,000 shares in DEF Ltd (transferred into the trust at a CGT value of £27,000 but now valued at only £13,000).

On 30 June 2003, the trustees had sold shares in GHK Ltd at a gain of £3,000 (after deducting indexation allowance to April 1998). On 7 July 2003, they sold shares in LMN Ltd at a loss of £500. None of the above-mentioned trust investments were business assets for taper relief purposes. At 6 April 2003, the trustees had allowable capital losses of £1,000 brought forward from earlier years.

In December 2003, F sells the ABC Ltd shares for £11,600. He also disposes of other assets in 2003/04 realising chargeable gains of £9,400 (with no taper relief due). In 2006/07, he sells the DEF Ltd shares for £15,700 and also disposes of other assets realising chargeable gains of £19,000 (all attracting 35% taper relief) and allowable losses of £1,500.

F takes over entitlement to trust losses as follows

	£	£
Loss on DEF Ltd shares transferred to F £(27,000 – 13,000)		14,000
Deduct Trustees' 'pre-entitlement gains'*:		
(i) gain on ABC Ltd shares transferred to F	5,000	
(ii) other gains in period 6.4.02–18.9.02	3,000	8,000
Loss treated as accruing to F (note (a))		£6,000

* See *TCGA 1992, s 71(2A)*

225.5 Settlements

F's CGT position for 2003/04 and 2006/07 is as follows

2003/04

	£
Gain on sale of ABC Ltd shares £(11,600 − 11,000)	600
Other gains	9,400
	10,000
Deduct Annual exemption	7,900
Gains chargeable to tax 2002/03	£2,100
Ex-trust losses carried forward	£6,000

2005/06

	£	£
Gain on sale of DEF Ltd shares £(15,700 − 13,000)	2,700	
Deduct Ex-trust losses brought forward and treated as a loss for the year	2,700	—
Other gains	19,000	
Deduct Losses for the year	1,500	
	17,500	
Deduct Taper relief @ 35%	6,125	11,375
		11,375
Deduct Annual exemption		8,800
Gains chargeable to tax		£2,575

	£
Ex-trust losses brought forward	6,000
Utilised in 2006/07	2,700
Unused balance (note (*b*))	£3,300

Notes

(*a*) Trust losses of £1,000 brought forward and £500 accruing in 2002/03 cannot be transferred to F and in this case are wasted. The 'pre-entitlement gains' cannot be reduced by those losses before being set against the loss on DEF Ltd shares.

(*b*) In F's hands, the loss can only be set against a gain on the DEF Ltd shares on which it arose. As all those shares are sold in 2006/07, the loss cannot be carried forward any further and the unused balance of £3,300 is written off.

225.6 **TERMINATION OF INTEREST IN POSSESSION ON DEATH** [*TCGA 1992, s 72; FA 2006, Sch 12 para 30(2)*]

(A)

K is entitled to an interest in possession under a settlement. The settled property consists of shares and cash. On K's death, L is entitled to a life interest in succession to K. K dies on 1 December 2006, when the shares are valued at £200,000. The trustees' allowable cost in respect of the shares is £40,000.

On K's death, the trustees are deemed to have disposed of and immediately reacquired the shares for £200,000, thus uplifting the CGT base cost, but no chargeable gain then arises.

Note

(*a*)   Where the deceased became entitled to the interest in possession on or after 22 March 2006, the above treatment applies only if

(i)   the deceased died under the age of 18 and, immediately before his death, *IHTA 1984, s 71D* (age 18 to 25 trusts) applies to the property in which the interest subsists; or

(ii)   immediately before his death,

(*a*)   the interest in possession is an immediate post-death interest within *IHTA 1984, s 49A*;

(*b*)   the interest is a transitional serial interest within *IHTA 1984, s 49C*;

(*c*)   the interest is a disabled person's interest within *IHTA 1984, s 89B(1)(c)(d)*; or

(*d*)   *IHTA 1984, s 71A* (trusts for bereaved minors) applies to the property in which the interest subsists.

[*TCGA 1992, s 72(1)–(1C); FA 2006, Sch 20 para 30(2)*].

(B)

In 1976, E created a settlement for the benefit of his children M and N and his grandchildren, transferring an investment property valued at £10,000 to the trustees. The terms of the settlement were that M and N each have a life interest in half of the trust income, with the remainder passing to E's grandchildren. In 1990, N assigned his interest to P, an unrelated party, for £35,000, its then market value. In 2006, N dies. The value of a half share of the trust property is then £65,000.

On N's death, his life interest terminates. There is no effect on the trustees as N was no longer the person entitled to the life interest within the meaning of *TCGA 1992, s 72*.

Notes

(*a*)   No chargeable gain arises on the disposal by N of his interest. [*TCGA 1992, s 76*].

(*b*)   P may claim an allowable loss on extinction of the interest. For an example of the computation if the interest is a wasting asset, see 229.3 WASTING ASSETS.

226   Shares and Securities

Cross-references. See also 204 ASSETS HELD ON 6 APRIL 1965, 205 ASSETS HELD ON 31 MARCH 1982, 212 INDEXATION, 223 QUALIFYING CORPORATE BONDS and 227 SHARES AND SECURITIES — IDENTIFICATION RULES.

226.1   REORGANISATION OF SHARE CAPITAL — VALUATION OF DIFFERENT CLASSES OF SHARE ON SUBSEQUENT DISPOSAL [TCGA 1992, ss 126–131]

(A) Unquoted shares

V acquired 10,000 ordinary shares in X Ltd, an unquoted trading company, in April 1997 at a cost of £15,000. In April 2002, as part of a reorganisation of share capital, V was additionally allotted 3,000 new 9% preference shares in X Ltd for which he paid £3,900. In June 2006, V sold his ordinary shareholding, in an arm's length transaction, for £20,000, but retained his preference shares, then valued at £4,000. The indexation factor for the period April 1997 to April 1998 (see note (b)) is 0.040.

The chargeable gain on the disposal of the ordinary shares is calculated as follows

	£
Disposal consideration	20,000
Cost (£15,000 + £3,900) $\times \dfrac{20,000}{20,000 + 4,000}$	15,750
Unindexed gain	4,250
Indexation allowance $\dfrac{15,000}{18,900} \times £15,750 \times 0.040$	500
Chargeable gain 2006/07 (subject to TAPER RELIEF (228))	£3,750
Allowable cost of 3,000 preference shares (£15,000 + £3,900 − £15,750)	3,150
Indexation allowance to April 1998 $\dfrac{15,000}{18,900} \times £3,150 \times 0.040$	100
Indexed cost	£3,250

Notes

(a)   The ordinary shares and preference shares held after the reorganisation (the 'new holding') constitute a single asset. [TCGA 1992, s 127]. A disposal of part of the new holding is thus a part disposal. If neither class of shares comprising the new holding is quoted on a recognised stock exchange at any time not later than three months after the reorganisation, acquisition cost on a part disposal is apportioned by reference to market values at the date of disposal. [TCGA 1992, s 129].

(b)   Other than for the purposes of corporation tax on chargeable gains, indexation allowance is frozen at its April 1998 level. Therefore, the indexation factor for April 1998 is used in respect of disposals in a later month (and expenditure incurred in April 1998 or later does not attract indexation allowance at all). See 212 INDEXATION.

(B) Quoted shares

Assume the facts to be as in (A) above except that both the ordinary and preference shares are quoted on a recognised stock exchange. On the first day of dealing after the reorganisation took effect, the ordinary shares were quoted at £1.85 and the preference shares at £1.35. V's holdings were therefore valued at £18,500 and £4,050 respectively.

The chargeable gain on the disposal of the ordinary shares is calculated as follows

	£
Disposal consideration	20,000
Cost (£15,000 + £3,900) $\times \dfrac{18,500}{18,500 + 4,050}$	15,506
Unindexed gain	4,494
Indexation allowance $\dfrac{15,000}{18,900} \times £15,506 \times 0.040$	492
Chargeable gain 2006/07 (subject to TAPER RELIEF (228))	£4,002
Allowable cost of 3,000 preference shares (£15,000 + £3,900 − £15,506)	3,394
Indexation allowance to April 1998 $\dfrac{15,000}{18,900} \times £3,394 \times 0.040$	108
Indexed cost	£3,502

Note

(a)   Where one or more of the classes of shares or debentures comprising the new holding is quoted on a recognised stock exchange at any time not later than three months after the reorganisation, acquisition cost on a part disposal is apportioned by reference to market values on the first day of dealing on which the prices quoted reflect the reorganisation. [*TCGA 1992, s 130*].

226.1　Shares and Securities

(C) Quoted shares — reorganisation after 31 March 1982, original holding acquired on or before that date

In 1980, W subscribed for 5,000 £1 ordinary shares at par in L plc, a quoted company. The value of his holding at 31 March 1982 was £8,000. In November 1990, L plc offered ordinary shareholders two 7% preference shares at £1 per share in respect of each five ordinary shares held. W took up his entitlement of 2,000 preference shares. On the first day of dealing after the reorganisation, the ordinary shares were quoted at £3.00 (making W's holding worth £15,000) and the preference shares at £1.02 (valuing W's holding at £2,040). In June 2006, W sells his preference shares on the market at £1.40 (total proceeds £2,800). (For simplicity, costs of acquisition and disposal are ignored in this example.) The indexation factor from March 1982 to April 1998 is 1.047 and from November 1990 to April 1998 it is 0.251.

The gain on the disposal of the preference shares is computed as follows

The calculation, without re-basing to 1982, is

	£
Disposal consideration	2,800
Cost (£5,000 + £2,000) × $\dfrac{2,040}{2,040 + 15,000}$	838
Unindexed gain	1,962
Indexation allowance (see below)	1,063
Gain after indexation	£899

The calculation, with re-basing to 1982, is

	£
Disposal consideration	2,800
(31.3.82 value £8,000 + cost £2,000) × $\dfrac{2,040}{2,040 + 15,000}$	1,197
Unindexed gain	1,603

Indexation allowance $\dfrac{8,000}{10,000} \times £1,197 \times 1.047 = £1,003$

$\dfrac{2,000}{10,000} \times £1,197 \times 0.251 = \underline{£60}$

	£
	1,063
Gain after indexation	£540
Chargeable gain 2006/07 (subject to TAPER RELIEF (228))	£540

Note

(a)　On a subsequent disposal of the ordinary shares, their cost would be £6,162 (£5,000 + £2,000 − £838) or, if re-basing applied, £8,803 (£8,000 + £2,000 − £1,197). In either case, indexation would be based on £8,803.

226.2 **BONUS ISSUES** [*TCGA 1992, ss 126–128, 130*]

(A) Bonus of same class
In October 1993, Y plc made a scrip issue of one ordinary share for every 10 held. L held 5,000 ordinary shares, which he acquired in May 1986 for £5,500, and therefore received 500 shares in the bonus issue. In October 2006, L sells 3,000 of his shares for £7,000. The indexation factor for the period May 1986 to April 1998 (see note (*a*)) is 0.662.

Section 104 **holding**	Shares	Qualifying expenditure £	Indexed pool £
May 1986 acquisition	5,000	5,500	5,500
October 1993 bonus issue	500		
Indexed rise: May 1986 – April 1998			
£5,500 × 0.662			3,641
	5,500	5,500	9,141
October 2006 disposal	(3,000)	(3,000)	(4,986)
Pool carried forward	2,500	£2,500	£4,155

Calculation of chargeable gain	£
Disposal consideration	7,000
Allowable cost $\frac{3,000}{5,500} \times £5,500$	3,000
Unindexed gain	4,000
Indexation allowance	
$\frac{3,000}{5,500} \times £9,141 = £4,986$	
£4,986 − £3,000	1,986
Chargeable gain 2006/07 (subject to TAPER RELIEF (228))	£2,014

Note
(*a*)   Other than for the purposes of corporation tax on chargeable gains, indexation allowance is frozen at its April 1998 level. Therefore, the indexation factor for April 1998 is used in respect of disposals in a later month (and expenditure incurred in April 1998 or later does not attract indexation allowance at all). See 212 INDEXATION.

The indexed pool is upgraded as if the entire holding had been disposed of at the end of 5 April 1998 but is not adjusted for any subsequent indexed rise in expenditure. [*TCGA 1992, s 110A; FA 1998, s 125(2)(4)(5)*].

(B) Bonus of different class

At various dates after 5 April 1982 and before 6 April 1985, R bought a total of 2,000 'A' shares in T plc for £3,800. The value of the indexed pool immediately before 6 April 1985 was £4,460. In June 1989, R bought a further 500 'A' shares for £800. In October 1993 T plc made a bonus issue of 2 'B' shares for each 5 'A' shares held, and R received 1,000 'B' shares, valued at £1.20 each (total value £1,200) on the first dealing day after the issue. On the same day, the 'A' shares were quoted at £2 each (total value £5,000). In December 2006 R sells his 1,000 'B' shares for £2,000.

Indexation factors	April 1985 to June 1989	0.218
	June 1989 to October 1993	0.229
	October 1993 to April 1998 (note (c))	0.147

Section 104 holding – 'A' shares

	Shares	Qualifying expenditure £	Indexed pool £
Pool at 6.4.85	2,000	3,800	4,460
Indexed rise: April 1985 to June 1989 £4,460 × 0.218			972
June 1989 acquisition	500	800	800
	2,500	4,600	6,232
Indexed rise: June 1989 to October 1993 £6,232 × 0.229			1,427
	2,500	4,600	7,659
October 1993 bonus issue of 'B' shares: transfer proportion of expenditure and indexed pool to 'B' shares (see note (a))		(890)	(1,482)
	2,500	3,710	6,177
Indexed rise: October 1993 to April 1998 £6,177 × 0.147			908
Pool of 'A' shares carried forward	2,500	£3,710	£7,085

Section 104 holding — 'B' shares

October 1993 bonus issue: proportion of pools transferred from 'A' shares holding	1,000	890	1,482
Indexed rise: October 1993 to April 1998 £1,482 × 0.147			218
	1,000	890	1,700
December 2006 disposal	1,000	890	1,700
	—	—	—

Calculation of chargeable gain on disposal of 'B' shares

	£
Disposal consideration	2,000
Allowable cost (as allocated)	890
Unindexed gain	1,110
Indexation allowance £1,700 − £890	810
Chargeable gain 2006/07 (subject to TAPER RELIEF (228))	£300

Notes

(a)   The cost of the 'A' shares is apportioned between 'A' and 'B' shares by reference to market values on the first day of dealing after the reorganisation. The indexed pool is apportioned in the same way.

Proportion of qualifying expenditure $£4,600 \times \dfrac{1,200}{1,200 + 5,000}$ £890

Proportion of indexed pool $£7,659 \times \dfrac{1,200}{1,200 + 5,000}$ £1,482

(HMRC Capital Gains Manual CG 51965 et seq.).

(b)   A different basis of apportionment applies to unquoted shares (see HMRC Capital Gains Manual CG 51919 et seq.).

(c)   Other than for the purposes of corporation tax on chargeable gains, indexation allowance is frozen at its April 1998 level. Therefore, the indexation factor for April 1998 is used in respect of disposals in a later month (and expenditure incurred in April 1998 or later does not attract indexation allowance at all). See 212 INDEXATION.

The indexed pool is upgraded as if the entire holding had been disposed of at the end of 5 April 1998 but is not adjusted for any subsequent indexed rise in expenditure. [*TCGA 1992, s 110A; FA 1998, s 125(2)(4)(5)*].

226.3   Shares and Securities

226.3 **RIGHTS ISSUES** [*TCGA 1992, s 42, s 123(1), s 128(4)*]

Cross-reference. See 226.8(B) below as regards sale of rights.

(A) Rights issue of same class
W plc is a quoted company which in June 1992 made a rights issue of one £1 ordinary share for every eight £1 ordinary shares held, at £1.35 payable on allotment. V, who held 16,000 £1 ordinary shares purchased in May 1984 for £15,000, took up his entitlement in full, and was allotted 2,000 shares. In December 2006, he sells 6,000 of his shares for £12,000.

Indexation factors	May 1984 to April 1985	0.065
	April 1985 to June 1992	0.470
	June 1992 to April 1998 (note (*a*))	0.167

Section 104 **holding**	Shares	Qualifying expenditure £	Indexed pool £
May 1984 acquisition	16,000	15,000	15,000
Indexed rise: May 1984 – April 1985			
£15,000 × 0.065			975
Pool at 6.4.85	16,000	15,000	15,975
Indexed rise: April 1985 – June 1992			
£15,975 × 0.470			7,508
June 1992 rights issue	2,000	2,700	2,700
	18,000	17,700	26,183
Indexed rise: June 1992 – April 1998			
£26,183 × 0.167			4,373
			30,556
December 2006 disposal	(6,000)	(5,900)	(10,185)
Pool carried forward	12,000	£11,800	£20,371

Calculation of chargeable gain	£
Disposal consideration	12,000
Allowable cost $\frac{6,000}{18,000} \times £17,700$	5,900
Unindexed gain	6,100
Indexation allowance	

$$\frac{6,000}{18,000} \times £30,556 = £10,185$$

	£
£10,185 – £5,900	4,285
Chargeable gain 2006/07 (subject to TAPER RELIEF (228))	£1,815

Note
(*a*)   Other than for the purposes of corporation tax on chargeable gains, indexation allowance is frozen at its April 1998 level. See 212 INDEXATION.

The indexed pool is upgraded as if the entire holding had been disposed of at the end of 5 April 1998 but is not adjusted for any subsequent indexed rise in expenditure. [*TCGA 1992, s 110A; FA 1998, s 125(2)(4)(5)*].

(B) Rights issue of different class

On 1 March 1992, A acquired 6,000 quoted £1 ordinary shares in S plc at a cost of £7,800. In October 1995, S plc made a rights issue of one 50p 'B' share for every five £1 ordinary shares held, at 60p payable in full on application. A took up his entitlement in full, acquiring 1,200 'B' shares. On the first dealing day after issue, the 'B' shares were quoted at 65p and the £1 ordinary shares at £1.50. A sells his 'B' shares in December 2006 for £2,000.

Indexation factors	March 1992 to October 1995	0.096
	October 1995 to April 1998	0.085

Section 104 holding — ordinary shares	Shares	Qualifying expenditure £	Indexed pool £
Acquisition 1.3.92	6,000	7,800	7,800
Indexed rise: March 1992 to October 1995 £7,800 × 0.096			749
October 1995 rights issue of 'B' shares	—	720	720
	6,000	8,520	9,269
Transfer proportion of expenditure and indexed pool to 'B' shares (note (*a*))		(680)	(739)
	6,000	7,840	8,530
Indexed rise: October 1995 to April 1998 £8,530 × 0.085			725
Pool of ordinary shares carried forward	6,000	£7,840	£9,255

Section 104 holding — 'B' shares			
October 1995 rights issue: proportion of pools transferred from ordinary shares holding	1,200	680	739
Indexed rise: October 1995 to April 1998 £739 × 0.085			63
	1,200	680	802
December 2006 disposal	(1,200)	(680)	(802)
	—	—	—

Calculation of chargeable gain on disposal of 'B' shares	£
Disposal consideration	2,000
Allowable cost (as allocated)	680
Unindexed gain	1,320
Indexation allowance £802 − £680	122
Chargeable gain 2006/07 (subject to TAPER RELIEF (228))	£1,198

226.3   Shares and Securities

Notes

(*a*)   The cost of the original shares is apportioned between the original shares and the 'B' shares by reference to market values on the first day of dealing after the reorganisation. The indexed pool is apportioned in the same way.

Proportion of qualifying expenditure

$$£8,520 \times \frac{1,200 \times 0.65}{(1,200 \times 0.65) + (6,000 \times 1.50)} \qquad \underline{£680}$$

Proportion of indexed pool

$$£9,269 \times \frac{1,200 \times 0.65}{(1,200 \times 0.65) + (6,000 \times 1.50)} \qquad \underline{£739}$$

(HMRC Capital Gains Manual CG 51965 et seq.).

(*b*)   A different basis of apportionment applies to unquoted shares (see HMRC Capital Gains Manual CG 51919 et seq.).

(C) Rights issue of same class: disposal out of *section 104* holding and 1982 holding

G has purchased 100,000 25p ordinary shares in C plc as follows

Date	Number of shares acquired	Cost £
22.5.80	20,000	0.78
5.11.83	15,000	1.10
14.9.84	40,000	1.00
30.4.02	25,000	2.30

In May 1992, C made a rights issue of one ordinary share for every five held, at £1.50 payable in full on application. G took up his rights in full (15,000 ordinary shares). He sells 105,000 shares in August 2006 for £2.50 per share. The shares were quoted at 90p on 31 March 1982. They are a non-business asset for taper relief purposes. Incidental costs of acquisition and disposal are disregarded for the purposes of this example.

Indexation factors		
	March 1982 to April 1998	1.047
	November 1983 to April 1985	0.094
	September 1984 to April 1985	0.052
	April 1985 to May 1992	0.470
	May 1992 to April 1998	0.167

Section 104 **holding**	Shares	Qualifying expenditure £	Indexed pool £
5.11.83 acquisition	15,000	16,500	16,500
Indexed rise: November 1983 to April 1985			
£16,500 × 0.094			1,551
14.9.84 acquisition	40,000	40,000	40,000
Indexed rise: September 1984 to April 1985			
£40,000 × 0.052			2,080
Pool at 6.4.85	55,000	56,500	60,131
Indexed rise: April 1985 to May 1992			
£60,131 × 0.470			28,262
May 1992 rights issue	11,000	16,500	16,500
	66,000	73,000	104,893
Indexed rise: May 1992 to April 1998			
£104,893 × 0.167			17,517
	66,000	73,000	122,410
August 2006 disposal	(66,000)	(73,000)	(122,410)
	—	—	—

1982 holding	Shares	Cost £	Market value 31.3.82 £
22.5.80 acquisition	20,000	15,600	18,000
May 1992 rights issue (note (*a*))	4,000	6,000	6,000
	24,000	21,600	24,000
August 2006 disposal	(14,000)	(12,600)	(14,000)
Pool carried forward	10,000	£9,000	£10,000

Calculation of chargeable gain

(i) Identify 25,000 shares sold with shares acquired on 30 April 2002.

	£
Disposal consideration 25,000 × £2.50	62,500
Allowable cost 25,000 × £2.30	57,500
Chargeable gain (subject to TAPER RELIEF (228))	£5,000

(ii) Identify 66,000 shares sold with *section 104* holding

	£
Disposal consideration 66,000 × £2.50	165,000
Allowable cost	73,000
Unindexed gain	92,000
Indexation allowance £122,410 − £73,000	49,410
Chargeable gain (subject to TAPER RELIEF (228))	£42,590

(iii) Identify 14,000 shares with 1982 holding

Without re-basing to 1982

	£
Disposal consideration $14,000 \times £2.50$	35,000
Cost $\dfrac{14,000}{24,000} \times £21,600$	12,600
Unindexed gain	22,400
Indexation allowance (see below)	11,579
Gain after indexation	£10,821

With re-basing to 1982

	£	£
Disposal consideration		35,000
Allowable expenditure $\dfrac{14,000}{24,000} \times £24,000$		14,000
Unindexed gain		21,000
Indexation allowance		
$£14,000 \times \dfrac{18,000}{24,000} \times 1.047$	10,994	
$£14,000 \times \dfrac{6,000}{24,000} \times 0.167$	585	
		11,579
Gain after indexation		£9,421
Chargeable gain (subject to TAPER RELIEF (228))		£9,421

Total pre-tapered gain 2006/07 £5,000 + £42,590 + £9,421   £57,011

Notes

(a)   The 1982 holding cannot be increased by an 'acquisition', but can be increased by a rights issue as this is not treated as involving an acquisition. [*TCGA 1992, s 109(2), ss 127, 128*].

(b)   Other than for the purposes of corporation tax on chargeable gains, disposals after 5 April 1998 are identified firstly with shares acquired on the same day, next with acquisitions in the following 30 days, then on a LIFO basis with post-5 April 1998 acquisitions as in (i) above, then with the '*section 104* holding' at 5 April 1998 as in (ii) above, then with the '1982 holding' as in (iii) above, and then on a LIFO basis with acquisitions on or before 6 April 1965. [*TCGA 1992, ss 105, 106A*].

226.4 **EXCHANGE OF SECURITIES FOR THOSE IN ANOTHER COMPANY** [*TCGA 1992, ss 135, 137, 138; FA 2002, s 45, Sch 9 paras 1, 7*]

(A) Takeover by quoted company

S was a shareholder in N Ltd, an unquoted company. He subscribed for his 20,000 50p ordinary shares at 60p per share in 1979 and the shares were valued at £3 each at 31 March 1982. In July 1987, the shareholders accepted an offer by a public company, M plc, for their shares. Each ordinary shareholder received one £1 ordinary M plc share plus 45p cash for every two N Ltd shares held. S acquired 10,000 M plc shares and received cash of £4,500. The M plc shares were valued at £7.50 each at the time of the acquisition. On 25 April 2006, S sells 4,000 of his 10,000 M plc shares for £54,000.

Indexation factors	March 1982 to July 1987	0.281
	March 1982 to April 1998	1.047

(i) On the merger in 1987/88, S makes a disposal only to the extent that he receives cash

	£
Disposal consideration	4,500
Allowable cost $\dfrac{4,500}{4,500 + (10,000 \times £7.50 = £75,000)} \times £12,000$	679
Unindexed gain	3,821
Indexation allowance £679 × 0.281	191
Chargeable gain 1987/88	£3,630

Note

(*a*) The fraction applied to allowable cost corresponds to 5.66%. If the percentage had not exceeded 5% the cash distribution of £4,500 would have been regarded as 'small' and could have been deducted from allowable cost (Revenue Tax Bulletin November 1992 p 46). [*TCGA 1992, s 122*]. No gain would then have arisen in 1987/88, but the allowable cost would have been reduced by £4,500. See also 226.8(B) below. (A distribution made after 23 February 1997 can additionally be regarded as 'small' if it does not exceed £3,000 — Revenue Tax Bulletin February 1997 p 397.)

(ii) The chargeable gain on disposal in 2006/07 is

Without re-basing to 1982

	£
Consideration for disposal of M plc shares	54,000
Allowable cost $(12,000 - 679) \times \dfrac{4,000}{10,000}$	4,528
Unindexed gain	49,472
Indexation allowance (see below)	23,706
Gain after indexation	£25,766

226.4   Shares and Securities

With re-basing to 1982

	£
Disposal consideration (as above)	54,000
Market value 31.3.82	

$$£(20,000 \times £3) \times \frac{75,000}{75,000 + 4,500} \times \frac{4,000}{10,000} \qquad \text{(note } (b)) \qquad 22,642$$

Unindexed gain	31,358
Indexation allowance £22,642 × 1.047	23,706
Gain after indexation	£7,652
Chargeable gain 2006/07 (subject to TAPER RELIEF (228))	£7,652

Notes

(a)   The M plc shares are regarded as the same asset as the original N Ltd shares. [*TCGA 1992, ss 127, 135*]. Re-basing to 31 March 1982 can thus apply, as the original shares were held on that date.

(b)   Where there has been a part disposal after 31 March 1982 and before 6 April 1988 of an asset held on the earlier of those dates, and this is followed by a disposal after 5 April 1988 to which re-basing applies, the re-basing rules are deemed to have applied to the part disposal. [*TCGA 1992, Sch 3 para 4(1)*].

(B) Takeover by unquoted company

Y Ltd, a small unquoted company, is taken over in June 1996 by another unquoted company, C Ltd. The terms of the acquisition are that holders of £1 ordinary shares in Y Ltd receive two £1 ordinary shares and one £1 deferred share in C Ltd in exchange for every two ordinary shares held.

B acquired his holding of 500 Y Ltd shares on the death of his wife in May 1992, at probate value of £10,000. In May 2006, B sells his 250 C Ltd deferred shares for £4,500. The value of his 500 C Ltd ordinary shares is then £25,000. The indexation factor for May 1992 to April 1998 is 0.167.

There is no CGT disposal in 1996/97. The chargeable gain on the 2006/07 disposal is calculated as follows

	£
Disposal consideration	4,500

$$\text{Allowable cost } \frac{4,500}{4,500 + 25,000} \times £10,000 \qquad 1,525$$

Unindexed gain	2,975
Indexation allowance £1,525 × 0.167	255
Chargeable gain 2006/07 (subject to TAPER RELIEF (228))	£2,720
The allowable cost carried forward of the 500 C Ltd ordinary shares is (£10,000 − £1,525)	£8,475

(C) Earn-outs

K owns 10,000 ordinary shares in M Ltd, which he acquired for £12,000 in December 2000. In July 2006, the whole of the issued share capital of M Ltd was acquired by P plc. Under the terms of the takeover, K receives £2 per share plus the right to further consideration up to a maximum of £1.50 per share depending on future profit performance. The initial consideration is receivable in cash, but the deferred consideration is to be satisfied by the issue of shares in P plc. In December 2007, K duly receives 2,000 ordinary shares valued at £6 per share in full settlement of his entitlement. The right to future consideration is valued at £1.40 per share in July 2006.

If K elects to disapply *TCGA 1992, s 138A* **the position would be**

2006/07

	£	£
Disposal proceeds 10,000 × £2	20,000	
Value of rights 10,000 × £1.40	14,000	34,000
Cost		12,000
Chargeable gain 2006/07 (subject to TAPER RELIEF (228))		£22,000

2007/08

	£
Disposal of rights to deferred consideration:	
Proceeds — 2,000 P plc shares @ £6	12,000
Deemed cost of acquiring rights	14,000
Allowable loss 2007/08	£2,000
Cost for CGT purposes of 2,000 P plc shares	£12,000

Without an election, the position would be

2006/07

	£
Proceeds (cash) (as above)	20,000
Cost £12,000 × $\dfrac{20,000}{20,000 + 14,000}$	7,059
Chargeable gain 2006/07 (subject to TAPER RELIEF (228))	£12,941
Cost of earn-out right for CGT purposes (£12,000 − £7,059)	£4,941

2007/08

The shares in P plc stand in the place of the right to deferred consideration and will be regarded as having been acquired in December 2000 for £4,941. No further gain or loss arises until a disposal of the shares takes place.

226.4 Shares and Securities

Notes

(a) Under *TCGA 1992, s 138A* the right to deferred consideration (the 'earn-out right') is treated as a security within *TCGA 1992, s 132*. The gain on the original shares (to the extent that it does not derive from cash consideration) can then be held over against the value of the new shares. For rights conferred before 10 April 2003, an election must be made by the vendor for this treatment to apply. For rights conferred on or after that date, treatment as a security is automatic where the conditions are satisfied, subject to the right to elect for such treatment not to apply. [*TCGA 1992, s 138A; FA 1997, s 89; FA 2003, s 161*].

(b) Various conditions must be satisfied for *section 138A* treatment to apply. In particular, the value or quantity of the securities to be received as deferred consideration must be 'unascertainable' (as defined). Any right to receive cash and/or an ascertainable amount of securities as part of the deferred consideration does not fall within these provisions and must be distinguished from the earn-out right, though this does not prevent these provisions from applying to the earn-out right.

(c) See 206.2 CAPITAL SUMS DERIVED FROM ASSETS above for deferred consideration generally.

226.5 SCHEMES OF RECONSTRUCTION [*TCGA 1992, s 136; FA 2002, s 45, Sch 9 paras 2, 7*]

N Ltd carried on a manufacturing and wholesaling business. In 1996, it was decided that the wholesaling business should be carried on by a separate company. Revenue clearance under *TCGA 1992, s 138* was obtained, and a company, R Ltd, was formed which, in consideration for the transfer to it by N Ltd of the latter's wholesaling undertaking, issued shares to the shareholders of N Ltd. Each holder of ordinary shares in N Ltd additionally received one ordinary share in R Ltd for each N Ltd share he held. W, who purchased his 2,500 N shares for £10,000 in December 1991, received 2,500 R shares. None of the shares involved is quoted. In August 2006, W sells 1,500 of his N shares for £6 each, a total of £9,000, agreed to be their market value. The value of W's remaining 1,000 N shares is also £6 per share, and the value of his R shares is £4.50 per share. The indexation factor for the period December 1991 to April 1998 is 0.198.

	£
Disposal consideration	9,000
Allowable cost £10,000 × $\dfrac{9,000}{9,000 + (1,000 \times £6) + (2,500 \times £4.50)}$	3,429
Unindexed gain	5,571
Indexation allowance £3,429 × 0.198	679
Chargeable gain 2006/07 (subject to TAPER RELIEF (228))	£4,892

226.6 CONVERSION OF SECURITIES [*TCGA 1992, s 132*]

N bought £10,000 8% convertible loan stock in S plc, a quoted company, in June 1991. The cost was £9,800. In August 1996, N exercised his right to convert the loan stock into 'B' ordinary shares of the company, on the basis of 50 shares for £100 loan stock, and acquired 5,000 shares. In June 2006, N sells 3,000 of the shares for £5.00 each. The indexation factor for June 1991 to April 1998 is 0.213.

	£
Disposal consideration	15,000
Cost $\dfrac{3,000}{5,000} \times £9,800$	5,880
Unindexed gain	9,120
Indexation allowance £5,880 × 0.213	1,252
Chargeable gain 2006/07 (subject to TAPER RELIEF (228))	£7,868

Notes

(*a*)   The shares acquired on the conversion in 1996 stand in the shoes of the original loan stock. [*TCGA 1992, s 132*].

(*b*)   The loan stock cannot be a corporate bond (and thus cannot be a qualifying corporate bond) as it is convertible into securities other than corporate bonds, i.e. into ordinary shares. [*ICTA 1988, Sch 18 para 1(5); TCGA 1992, s 117(1)*].

226.7 **SCRIP DIVIDENDS** [*TCGA 1992, ss 141, 142; ICTA 1988, ss 249, 251(2)–(4)*]

D holds ordinary 20p shares in PLC, a quoted company. The company operates a scrip dividend (also known as a stock dividend) policy whereby shareholders are given the option to take dividends in cash or in new fully-paid ordinary 20p shares, the option being exercisable separately in relation to each dividend. D purchased 2,000 shares for £1,500 in March 1980 and a further 3,000 shares for £8,100 in May 1992 and up until the end of 1997 he has always taken cash dividends. In January 1998, he opts for a scrip dividend and receives 25 shares instead of a cash dividend of £100. On 20 April 2000, he purchases a further 1,000 shares for £3,950. He opts for cash dividends until in July 2000, he opts for a scrip dividend of 44 shares instead of a cash dividend of £180. He opts for cash dividends thereafter. In May 2006, he sells 2,069 shares for £8,550 (ex div), leaving himself with a holding of 4,000.

In the case of both scrip dividends taken by D, the market value of the new shares is equivalent to the cash dividend forgone. The 'appropriate amount in cash' (see *TCGA 1992, s 142*) is thus the amount of that dividend. [*ICTA 1988, s 251(2)*]. Relevant indexation factors are as follows.

May 1992 to January 1998	0.145
January 1998 to April 1998	0.019

The gain on the disposal in May 2006 is calculated as follows

(i) Identify 44 shares sold with those received by way of scrip dividend in July 2000 (LIFO) (note (*a*))

	£
Proceeds £8,550 × 44/2069	182
Cost (equal to 'appropriate amount in cash')	180
Chargeable gain (subject to TAPER RELIEF (228))	£2

(ii) Identify 1,000 shares sold with those acquired on 20 April 2000

	£
Proceeds £8,550 × 1,000/2,069	4,132
Cost	3,950
Chargeable gain (subject to TAPER RELIEF (228))	£182

(iii) Identify remaining 1,025 shares sold with '*section 104* holding' at 5 April 1998

Section 104 holding	Shares	Qualifying expenditure £	Indexed pool £
May 1992 acquisition	3,000	8,100	8,100
Indexed rise: May 1992 to January 1998 £8,100 × 0.145			1,175
	3,000	8,100	9,275
January 1998 scrip dividend 25 × 3,000/5,000 (note (*a*))	15	60	60
	3,015	8,160	9,335
Indexed rise: January 1998 to April 1998 £9,335 × 0.019			177
Pool at 5.4.98	3,015	8,160	9,512
May 2006 disposal	(1,025)	(2,775)	(3,234)
Pool carried forward	1,990	£5,385	£6,278

Proceeds £8,550 × 1,025/2,069	4,236
Cost £8,160 × 1,025/3,015	2,775
Unindexed gain	1,461
Indexation allowance £9,512 × 1,025/3,015 = £3,234	
£3,234 − £2,775	459
Chargeable gain (subject to TAPER RELIEF (228))	£1,002

Total pre-tapered gain 2006/07 (£2 + £182 + £1,002)	£1,186

The remaining holding of 4,000 shares consists of a '*section 104* holding' of 1,990 as illustrated above and a '1982 holding' of 2,010 (which was irrelevant to the May 2005 disposal) consisting of 2,000 purchased in March 1980 and 10 scrip dividend shares acquired in January 1998 and equated with the said purchase (see note (*a*)).

Notes

(*a*) Scrip dividends after 5 April 1998 are treated as free-standing acquisitions. Previously, a scrip dividend received by an individual was treated as a reorganisation within *TCGA 1992, s 128* so that the new shares equated with those already held. Thus, in this example, the January 1998 scrip dividend is split pro rata between the '1982 holding' and the '*section 104* holding'.

(*b*) See also 227.1 SHARES AND SECURITIES — IDENTIFICATION RULES.

226.8   Shares and Securities

226.8 CAPITAL DISTRIBUTIONS

(A) [*TCGA 1992, s 122*]

T holds 10,000 ordinary shares in a foreign company M SA. The shares were bought in April 1996 for £80,000. In February 2007, M SA has a capital reconstruction involving the cancellation of one-fifth of the existing ordinary shares in consideration of the repayment of £10 to each shareholder per share cancelled. T's holding is reduced to 8,000 shares, valued at £96,000. The indexation factor for the period April 1996 to April 1998 is 0.066.

	£
Disposal consideration (2,000 × £10)	20,000
Allowable cost $\dfrac{20,000}{20,000 + 96,000} \times £80,000$	13,793
Unindexed gain	6,207
Indexation allowance £13,793 × 0.066	910
Chargeable gain 2006/07 (subject to TAPER RELIEF (228))	£5,297
The allowable cost of the remaining shares is £80,000 − £13,793	£66,207

(B) Sale of rights [*TCGA 1992, ss 122, 123*]

X is a shareholder in K Ltd, owning 2,500 £1 ordinary shares which were purchased for £7,000 in October 1996. K Ltd makes a rights issue, but X sells his rights, without taking them up, for £700 in August 2006. The ex-rights value of X's 2,500 shares at the date of sale was £14,500. The indexation factor for the period October 1996 to April 1998 is 0.057.

'Section 104 holding' of K £1 ordinary shares	Shares	Qualifying expenditure £	Indexed pool £
October 1996 acquisition	2,500	7,000	7,000
Indexed rise to April 1998 £7,000 × 0.057			399
	2,500	£7,000	£7,399

HMRC cannot require the capital distribution to be treated as a disposal, as the £700 received for the rights does not exceed 5% of (£700 + £14,500) and in any case does not exceed £3,000 (see Revenue Tax Bulletin February 1997 p 397). [*TCGA 1992, s 122(2)*]. If the transaction is not treated as a disposal, the £700 is deducted from both the acquisition cost of the shares and the indexed pool, leaving balances of, respectively, £6,300 and £6,699. If the transaction is treated as a disposal (possibly because X wishes to utilise part of his annual exemption), the computation is as follows.

	£
Disposal proceeds	700
Allowable cost $\dfrac{700}{700 + 14,500} \times £7,000$	322
Unindexed gain	378
Indexation allowance £7,399 $\times \dfrac{700}{700 + 14,500} = £341$	
£341 − £322	19
Chargeable gain 2006/07 (subject to TAPER RELIEF (228))	£359

The allowable cost of the shares is then reduced to £6,678 (£7,000 − £322) and the balance on the indexed pool to £7,058 (£7,399 − £341).

227 Shares and Securities — Identification Rules

Cross-reference. See 226 SHARES AND SECURITIES.

227.1 IDENTIFICATION RULES AFTER 5 APRIL 1998 (OTHER THAN FOR CORPORATION TAX PURPOSES)

A has the following acquisitions/disposals of ordinary 25p shares in QED plc. Throughout their period of ownership by A, these shares are non-business assets for the purposes of TAPER RELIEF (228). QED ordinary 25p shares were worth 210p per share at 31 March 1982, and A has not made a global re-basing election (see 205 ASSETS HELD ON 31 MARCH 1982). In 2006/07, A made no disposals of chargeable assets other than as shown below.

Date	No. of shares bought/(sold)	Cost/(proceeds) £
1 May 1980	1,000	2,000
1 October 1983	2,000	4,500
1 December 1996	500	1,800
1 May 1999	(1,000)	(3,900)
25 May 1999	2,000	7,600
	4,500	
2 January 2000	(2,000)	(9,000)
1 July 2006	(2,000)	(12,000)
Remaining holding	500	

Relevant indexation factors are

March 1982 to April 1998 (note (*b*))	1.047
October 1983 to April 1985	0.097
April 1985 to December 1996	0.629
December 1996 to April 1998	0.053

(i) **The disposal on 1 May 1999** is matched with 1,000 of the shares acquired on 25 May 1999 (under the 30-day rule — see note (*a*)). The resulting chargeable gain is as follows.

	£
Proceeds 1.5.99	3,900
Cost (£7,600 × 1,000/2,000)	3,800
Chargeable gain (no taper relief due)	£100

(ii) **The disposal of 2,000 shares on 2 January 2000** is matched firstly with the remaining 1,000 acquired on 25 May 1999 (LIFO), and secondly with 1,000 of the 2,500 forming the '*section 104* holding' as follows.

	No. of shares	Qualifying expenditure £	Indexed pool £
Pool at 6.4.85	2,000	4,500	4,500
Indexation allowance to date:			
October 1983 – April 1985			
£4,500 × 0.097			437
	2,000	4,500	4,937
Indexed rise to December 1996:			
April 1985 – December 1996			
£4,937 × 0.629			3,105
Acquisition 1.12.96	500	1,800	1,800
	2,500	6,300	9,842
Indexed rise to April 1998:			
December 1996 – April 1998			
£9,842 × 0.053			522
	2,500	6,300	10,364
Disposal 2.1.2000	(1,000)	(2,520)	(4,146)
Pool carried forward	1,500	£3,780	£6,218

Chargeable gains are as follows.

	£	£
Proceeds 2.1.2000	4,500	4,500
Cost (£7,600 × 1,000/2,000)	3,800	
Cost (as above)		2,520
Unindexed gains	700	1,980
Indexation (£4,146 − £2,520)	—	1,626
Chargeable gains	£700	£354

Neither gain qualifies for taper relief. In each case, the shares acquired have been held for less than the requisite three complete years (for non-business asset taper relief) after 5 April 1998.

227.1 Shares and Securities — Identification Rules

(iii) **The disposal of 2,000 shares on 1 July 2006** is matched firstly with the remaining 1,500 in the '*section 104* holding', and secondly with 500 of the 1,000 shares forming the '1982 holding'.

Chargeable gains are as follows.

	£
Proceeds of 1,500 shares on 1.7.06	9,000
Cost (as per pool above)	3,780
Unindexed gain	5,220
Indexation (£6,218 − £3,780)	2,438
Chargeable gain subject to taper relief	2,782
Taper relief £2,782 × 35% (see below)	974
Chargeable gain	£1,808

	£	
Proceeds of 500 shares on 1.7.06	3,000	3,000
Cost (£2,000 × 500/1,000)	1,000	
Market value 31.3.82 500 × £2.10		1,050
Unindexed gain	2,000	1,950
Indexation to April 1998:		
£1,050 × 1.047	1,099	1,099
Gain after indexation	£901	£851

	£
Chargeable gain subject to taper relief	851
Taper relief £851 × 35% (see below)	298
Chargeable gain	£553

Taper relief is at 35% as the shares are non-business assets and have been held for eight plus one years since 5 April 1998, the one-year addition being by virtue of the fact that both the '*section 104* holding' and the '1982 holding' were acquired before 17 March 1998. [*TCGA 1992, s 2A(8)(9); FA 2000, s 66*].

Notes

(*a*) Other than for the purposes of corporation tax on chargeable gains, disposals after 5 April 1998 are identified (1) with shares acquired on the same day (with certain limited exceptions by election); (2) with acquisitions in the following 30 days; (3) on a LIFO basis with post-5 April 1998 acquisitions; (4) with the '*section 104* holding' at 5 April 1998; (5) with the '1982 holding'; (6) on a LIFO basis with acquisitions on or before 6 April 1965; (7) with shares acquired after the disposal (and after the expiry of the 30-day period in (2) above) taken in the order in which such acquisitions occur. [*TCGA 1992, ss 105, 105A, 105B, 106A; FA 2002, s 50(1)(2); FA 2006, s 74*].

(*b*) Other than for the purposes of corporation tax on chargeable gains, indexation allowance is frozen at its April 1998 level. See 212 INDEXATION.

The indexed pool is upgraded as if the entire holding had been disposed of at the end of 5 April 1998 but is not adjusted for any subsequent indexed rise in expenditure. [*TCGA 1992, s 110A; FA 1998, s 125(2)(4)(5)*].

227.2 **SHARE IDENTIFICATION RULES FOR COMPANIES** [*TCGA 1992, ss 104, 105–110; FA 2006, s 72*]

B Ltd has the following transactions in 25p ordinary shares of H plc, a quoted company. At no time did B Ltd's holding amount to 2% of H plc's issued shares.

		Cost/(proceeds) £
6.6.78	Purchased 500 at £0.85	425
3.11.81	Purchased 1,300 at £0.80	1,040
15.5.82	Purchased 1,000 at £1.02	1,020
8.9.82	Purchased 400 at £1.08	432
1.2.86	Purchased 1,200 at £1.14	1,368
29.7.87	Sold 2,000 at £1.30	(2,600)
8.6.90	Purchased 1,500 at £1.26	1,890
21.12.93	Received 1,000 from group company (cost £1,250, indexation to date £250)	1,500
10.5.06	Sold 3,900 at £2.50	(9,750)

The shares stood at £1.00 at 31.3.82.

Indexation factors	March 1982 to May 2006	1.489
	May 1982 to April 1985	0.161
	September 1982 to April 1985	0.158
	April 1985 to February 1986	0.019
	February 1986 to July 1987	0.054
	July 1987 to June 1990	0.245
	June 1990 to December 1993	0.120
	December 1993 to May 2006	0.393

Disposal on 10 May 2006

The 'section 104 holding' pool immediately prior to the disposal should be as follows

	Shares	Qualifying expenditure £	Indexed pool £
15.5.82 acquisition	1,000	1,020	1,020
Indexation to April 1985 £1,020 × 0.161			164
8.9.82 acquisition	400	432	432
Indexation to April 1985 £432 × 0.158			68
Pool at 6.4.85	1,400	1,452	1,684
Indexed rise: April 1985 – Feb. 1986 £1,684 × 0.019			32
1.2.86 acquisition	1,200	1,368	1,368
	2,600	2,820	3,084
Indexed rise: February 1986 – July 1987 £3,084 × 0.054			167
	2,600	2,820	3,251
29.7.87 disposal	(2,000)	(2,169)	(2,501)
c/f	£600	£651	£750

	Shares	Qualifying expenditure £	Indexed pool £
b/f	600	651	750
Indexed rise: July 1987 – June 1990			
£750 × 0.245			184
8.6.90 acquisition	1,500	1,890	1,890
	2,100	2,541	2,824
Indexed rise: June 1990 – December 1993			
£2,824 × 0.120			339
21.12.93 acquisition	1,000	1,250	1,500
	3,100	3,791	4,663
Indexed rise: December 1993 – May 2006			
£4,663 × 0.393			1,833
	3,100	3,791	6,546

The '1982 holding' is as follows

	Shares	Allowable expenditure £
6.6.78 acquisition	500	425
3.11.81 acquisition	1,300	1,040
	1,800	1,465

(i) Identify 3,100 shares sold with '*section 104* holding'	£
Disposal consideration 3,100 × £2.50	7,750
Allowable cost	3,791
Unindexed gain	3,959
Indexation allowance £6,546 − £3,791	2,755
Chargeable gain	£1,204

(ii) Identify 800 shares sold with '1982 holding'

	£	£
Disposal consideration 800 × £2.10	2,000	2,000
Cost $\dfrac{800}{1,800}$ × £1,465	651	
Market value 31.3.82 $\dfrac{800}{1,800}$ × £1,800		800
Unindexed gain	1,349	1,200
Indexation allowance £800 × 1.489	1,191	1,191
Gain after indexation	£158	£9
Chargeable gain		£9
Total chargeable gain 10 May 2006 (£1,204 + £9)		£1,213

Notes

(a) Share disposals by companies after 31.3.85 are identified firstly with the '*section 104* holding' and secondly with the '1982 holding', both of which are regarded as single assets.

(b) On share disposals after 5.4.88 identified with shares held at 31.3.82, the re-basing provisions have effect, and indexation is based on the higher of cost and 31.3.82 value. If an irrevocable election is made under *TCGA 1992, s 35(5)* for all assets to be treated as disposed of and re-acquired at their market value on 31.3.82, indexation must be based on the 31.3.82 value even if this is less than cost. [*TCGA 1992, s 55(1)(2)*].

(c) See also 207.2 COMPANIES.

228   Taper Relief

Cross-reference. See 227.1 SHARES AND SECURITIES — IDENTIFICATION RULES.

228.1   **THE BASIC RULES** [*TCGA 1992, s 2A, Sch A1; FA 2000, s 66; FA 2001, s 78, Sch 26; FA 2002, s 46; FA 2003, s 160*]

(A) Computing the tapered gain

Brett acquired an asset in 1996 for £20,000 and sells it in September 2006 for £40,000. He makes no other disposals in 2006/07. At no time after 5 April 1998 was the asset a business asset. The indexation factor from date of acquisition to April 1998 (see note (*a*)) is, say, 0.060.

The taxable gain is computed as follows

At the time of disposal, the asset has been held for eight complete years after 5 April 1998. Because it was acquired before 17 March 1998 and it is a non-business asset, a further one year is added. Using the table at *TCGA 1992, s 2A(5)*, the taper relief for a non-business asset held for nine complete years after 5 April 1998 is 35%.

	£
Proceeds	40,000
Less Cost of acquisition	20,000
Unindexed gain	20,000
Indexation to April 1998 £20,000 × 0.060	1,200
Chargeable gain	18,800
Less Taper relief £18,800 × 35%	6,580
Taxable gain subject to annual exemption	£12,220

Note

(*a*)   Other than for the purposes of corporation tax on chargeable gains, indexation allowance is frozen at its April 1998 level. Therefore, the indexation factor for April 1998 is used in respect of disposals in a later month (and expenditure incurred in April 1998 or later does not attract indexation allowance at all). See 212 INDEXATION.

(B) Set-off of losses

Hannah made four disposals in 2006/07, as follows.

On Asset A, she realised a chargeable gain of £15,000 (after indexation to April 1998). This asset was acquired in 1995 and sold in May 2006 and was a non-business asset throughout its ownership.

On Asset B, she realised a chargeable gain of £2,000. This asset was acquired in December 2003 and sold in October 2006 and was a non-business asset throughout its ownership.

On Asset C, she realised a chargeable gain of £9,500. This asset was acquired in August 2003 and sold in December 2006 and was a business asset throughout its ownership.

On Asset D, she realised an allowable loss of £6,000.

The gains qualify for taper relief as follows

Asset A was held for eight complete years after 5 April 1998 and qualifies for a one-year addition as it was acquired before 17 March 1998. The gain thus qualifies for 35% taper relief.

Asset B was held for less than the minimum period of ownership necessary for a gain on a non-business asset to qualify for taper relief (three complete years).

Asset C was held for three complete years. It thus qualifies for 75% taper relief.

The optimum set-off of losses is as follows

It is beneficial to offset the loss on Asset D firstly against the gain attracting no taper relief, i.e. the gain on Asset B, with the balance against the gain attracting the lower rate of taper relief, i.e. the gain on Asset A.

	£
Asset A	
Chargeable gain	15,000
Less Allowable loss (balance)	4,000
	11,000
Less Taper relief £11,000 × 35%	3,850
Tapered gain	£7,150
Asset B	
Chargeable gain	2,000
Less Allowable loss	2,000
Asset C	
Chargeable gain	9,500
Less Taper relief £9,500 × 75%	7,125
Tapered gain	£2,375
Total taxable gains subject to annual exemption	£9,525

Note

(a)   Both current year and brought forward losses are set against gains in such a way as to maximise the taper relief due. [*TCGA 1992, s 2A(6); FA 1998, s 121(1)*].

228.2　Taper Relief

228.2　**ASSETS WHICH ARE BUSINESS ASSETS FOR PART ONLY OF PERIOD OF OWNERSHIP** [*TCGA 1992, Sch A1 para 3*]

(A) General

Penny acquired a freehold property in March 1991 and sold it on 30 September 2007, realising a chargeable gain (after indexation to April 1998) of £95,000. Between March 1991 and September 2001 inclusive, the property was used as business premises and qualifies as a business asset for taper relief purposes. From October 2001 to September 2007 inclusive, it was let to a private non-trading tenant and was not a business asset. Penny made one other disposal in 2007/08, realising a loss of £10,000.

The gain is divided into two separate gains, which qualify for taper relief as follows

The relevant period of ownership for the purposes of taper relief is the 9.5 years from 6 April 1998 to 30 September 2007. During that period, the asset was a business asset for 3.5 years (April 1998 to September 2001) and a non-business asset for the remaining six years. Therefore, 3.5/9.5 of the gain (£35,000) qualifies for the business assets taper and 6/9.5 of the gain (£60,000) qualifies for the non-business assets taper.

The number of complete years in the qualifying holding period is nine. However, there is a one-year addition in the case of the non-business asset portion of the gain as the asset was acquired before 17 March 1998. [*TCGA 1992, s 2A(8)(9); FA 2000, s 66(3)(4)*].

The net taxable gains are computed as follows

	Business asset	Non-business asset	Total
	£	£	£
Chargeable gains	35,000	60,000	95,000
Deduct Allowable loss		10,000	10,000
Net chargeable gains	35,000	50,000	85,000
Deduct Taper relief @ 75%/40%	26,250	20,000	46,250
Taxable gains 2007/08 (subject to annual exemption)	£8,750	£30,000	£38,750

Notes

(*a*)　The gain on the freehold property, a mixed use asset, is treated for taper relief purposes as if it were two separate gains accruing on separate disposals of separate assets, one business and one non-business. [*TCGA 1992, Sch A1 para 3(5)*]. Of the two gains, the available loss is set against the one attracting the lower rate of taper relief (see 228.1(B) above and HMRC Capital Gains Manual CG 17976).

(*b*)　For a further example on change of use of an asset, see 228.3(A) below.

(B) Shares becoming a business asset on 6 April 2000 by virtue of FA 2000 [*TCGA 1992, Sch A1 paras 4, 6; FA 2000, s 67; FA 2001, s 78, Sch 26 para 3*]
In September 1995, Bob acquired by gift from his father 100 £1 ordinary shares in an unlisted family trading company, YOY Ltd, with an issued ordinary share capital of £1,000, each share carrying one vote. Bob's acquisition cost for CGT purposes, as reduced by a claim for business asset gifts hold-over relief, is £100.

On 12 June 1999, the company capitalises some of its reserves by means of a two for one bonus issue, increasing Bob's holding to 300 out of 3,000 shares.

On 6 April 2006, following a family dispute, Bob sells all his YOY shares to a cousin at their agreed market value of £19.03 per share, receiving £5,708. He makes one other disposal in 2006/07, realising a gain after taper relief of £20,000. The indexation factor for the period September 1995 to April 1998 is 0.080.

Throughout his ownership of the shares, Bob, who is otherwise self-employed, was on the company payroll but put in only a few hours per week.

The pre-tapered gain is computed as follows

	£
Proceeds	5,708
Deemed acquisition cost (September 1995)	100
Unindexed gain	5,608
Indexation allowance £100 × 0.080	8
Chargeable gain subject to taper relief	£5,600

The gain qualifies for taper relief as follows
The relevant period of ownership is the 8 years from 6 April 1998 to 6 April 2006. The bonus shares acquired in June 1999 are treated, by virtue of *TCGA 1992, s 127*, as the same asset as, and as acquired at the same time as, the original shares.

Throughout the period 6 April 1998 to 5 April 2000 (2 years), the shares are a non-business asset for taper relief purposes. YOY Ltd is not a qualifying company in relation to Bob; he can exercise at least 5% of the voting rights but less than 25% and he is not a 'full-time working officer or employee'. [*TCGA 1992, Sch A1 para 4(2), para 6(2)(3) as originally enacted*].

Throughout the period 6 April 2000 to 6 April 2006 (6 years), the shares are a business asset for taper relief purposes. YOY Ltd is a qualifying company in relation to Bob on any of the following counts (only one of which need be satisfied):

  (i)   it is an unlisted company;
  (ii) Bob is an employee of the company, albeit part-time;
  (iii) he can exercise at least 5% of the voting rights.

[*TCGA 1992, Sch A1 para 4(2), para 6(1), para 22(1); FA 2000, s 67(4)(5)(7)*].

Therefore, $\frac{2}{8}$ of the gain (£1,400) qualifies for taper relief at the non-business asset rate and $\frac{6}{8}$ (£4,200) at the business asset rate.

The number of complete years in the qualifying holding period (6.4.98–6.4.06) is eight. However, there is a one-year addition in the case of the non-business asset portion of the gain, as the shares were acquired before 17 March 1998. [*TCGA 1992, s 2A(8)(9); FA 2000, s 66(3)(4)*].

228.3 Taper Relief

The taxable gain is computed as follows

	Business asset	Non-business asset	Total
	£	£	£
Chargeable gain	4,200	1,400	5,600
Less Taper relief @ 75%/35%	3,150	490	3,640
Taxable gain	£1,050	£910	£1,960

Notes

(a) Amendments were made by *FA 2000, s 67* and by *FA 2001, Sch 26* to the definition of a business asset for taper relief purposes. These have effect for determining the status of an asset at any time after 5 April 2000. They do not affect the status of an asset at any time before 6 April 2000 even if that status falls to be determined as a result of a disposal on or after that date. [*FA 2000, s 67(7)*]. On the disposal of an asset which became a business asset on 6 April 2000 by virtue of the *FA 2000* or *FA 2001* changes, the gain must be apportioned using the rules illustrated in (A) above. Further changes are made by *FA 2003, s 160* to the definition with effect for determining the status of an asset after 5 April 2004. Where an asset becomes a business asset as a result of the changes, the gain must be apportioned for taper relief purposes in the same way as illustrated in this example.

(b) As the disposal took place after 5 April 2002 and the qualifying holding period consisted of at least two complete years, the whole of the business asset portion of the gain qualifies for taper relief at the maximum rate of 75%. [*TCGA 1992, s 2A(5); FA 2002, s 46*].

228.3 **TRANSFERS BETWEEN SPOUSES OR CIVIL PARTNERS** [*TCGA 1992, Sch A1 para 15; SI 2005 No 3229, Reg 123*]

Note. See 217.1 MARRIED PERSONS AND CIVIL PARTNERS as regards inter-spouse transfers generally.

(A) Assets other than shares and securities

Jack and Jill are a married couple living together. Jack owns a property which he acquired for residential letting in May 1996 for £60,000. On 7 April 2000, he gives the property to Jill who thereafter uses it as offices in her profession as a solicitor. Four years later, Jill decides to rent larger office premises and sells the property on 8 April 2006 for £110,000. She makes no other disposals in 2006/07. The indexation factor for the period May 1996 to April 1998 is 0.063.

Jack's disposal in 2000/01 is at no gain/no loss as follows

	£	£
Deemed consideration		63,780
Less: Cost of acquisition	60,000	
Indexation allowance £60,000 × 0.063	3,780	63,780
Gain/loss		Nil

The gain on Jill's disposal in 2006/07 is computed as follows

	£
Proceeds	110,000
Less Cost of acquisition (as above)	63,780
Chargeable gain subject to taper relief	46,220
Less Taper relief (see below)	30,043
Taxable gain subject to annual exemption	£16,177

The relevant period of ownership for taper relief purposes is the eight years from 6 April 1998 to 8 April 2006. During that period, the asset was a non-business asset for two years (6 April 1998 to 6 April 2000) and a business asset for six years (7 April 2000 to 8 April 2006). Therefore, two-eighths of the gain qualifies for non-business asset taper relief and six-eighths for business asset taper relief (see also 228.2 above) as follows.

The number of complete years in the qualifying holding period (6.4.98–8.4.06) is eight. However, there is a one-year addition in the case of the non-business asset portion of the gain, as the property was acquired before 17 March 1998. [*TCGA 1992, s 2A(8)(9); FA 2000, s 66(3)(4)*].

	£
(£46,220 × $\frac{2}{8}$ = £11,555) @ 35%	4,044
(£46,220 × $\frac{6}{8}$ = £34,665) @ 75%(maximum)	25,999
Total taper relief	£30,043

Notes

(*a*) Taper relief applies as if the time when the transferee spouse or civil partner acquired the asset was the time when the transferor spouse or civil partner acquired it.

(*b*) The question of whether an asset (other than shares or securities) was a business asset at any specified time in the combined period of ownership after 5 April 1998 is determined by reference to the use to which it was put by the spouse or civil partner holding it at that time.

(*c*) As regards that part of the combined period of ownership which falls *before* the transfer, the asset is also a business asset at any time if it then qualifies as such by reference to the spouse or civil partner to whom it is eventually transferred, i.e. where an asset owned by one spouse or civil partner is used in the other's business (not illustrated in this example).

228.3 Taper Relief

(B) Shares and securities

George and Kelly are a married couple living together. They each subscribed for and received 2,500 £1 shares at par (representing $2\frac{1}{2}\%$ of the voting rights) in Getrichquick. com plc when that company was floated on the London Stock Exchange on 30 April 2001. On 29 April 2004, Kelly gives her shares to George. On 30 April 2006, George sells his 5,000 shares for £25,000.

Throughout his ownership of Getrichquick.com shares, George is an employee of that company, but his wife is not.

Kelly's disposal in 2004/05 is for a deemed consideration of £2,500 thus producing no gain and no loss.

The gain on George's disposal in 2006/07 is computed as follows

	£
Proceeds (5,000 shares)	25,000
Less Cost of acquisition (£1 per share)	5,000
Chargeable gain subject to taper relief	20,000
Less Taper relief (£20,000 @ 75% — see below)	15,000
Taxable gain subject to annual exemption	£5,000

The relevant period of ownership is the five years to 30 April 2006. During the whole of that period, the company was a qualifying company by reference to George, by virtue of his being its employee. Therefore, the whole of the gain qualifies for business asset taper relief. The qualifying holding period is those same five years. Therefore, the gain qualifies in full for 75% business asset taper relief.

Notes

(*a*) Taper relief applies as if the time when the transferee spouse or civil partner acquired the asset was the time when the transferor spouse or civil partner acquired it.

(*b*) As regards shares and securities, the question of whether the asset was a business asset at any specified time in the combined period of ownership is determined only by reference to the individual making the ultimate disposal.

(*c*) If, instead, George had given his shares to Kelly and she made the ultimate sale, the gain would have qualified for business asset taper relief only from the date of the gift as only from that date would the company be a qualifying company by reference to her (due to her share of the voting rights then being 5%). The gain would have required apportionment using the method in (A) above.

228.4 **POSTPONED GAINS** [*TCGA 1992, Sch A1 para 16*]

Gordon disposes of shares in A Ltd, his family trading company, in August 2003, realising a chargeable gain (after indexation to April 1998) of £50,000. He had held the shares since 1989 and they qualified as a business asset for the purposes of taper relief. He acquires shares in a Venture Capital Trust in March 2004 for £60,000 and makes a claim for deferral relief under *TCGA 1992, Sch 5C* (see IT 28.3(B) VENTURE CAPITAL TRUSTS). He makes no other disposals in 2003/04 and wishes to leave sufficient gains in charge to cover his annual exemption.

The A Ltd shares were held for five complete years after 5 April 1998. The taper is therefore 75% (see the table at *TCGA 1992, s 2A(5) as amended by FA 2002, s 46*).

The gain is computed as follows

	£
Gain before taper relief	50,000
Less Deferred on reinvestment in VCT	
(optimum amount)	18,400*
	31,600
Less Taper relief £31,600 × 75%	23,700
Tapered gain for 2003/04 covered by annual exemption	£7,900

$$ * \ £7,900 \times \frac{100}{100 - 75} = £31,600. \ £50,000 - £31,600 = £18,400. $$

In June 2006, Gordon sells his VCT shares.

The deferred gain becomes chargeable in 2006/07 and is computed as follows

	£
Deferred gain before taper relief	18,400
Less Taper relief £18,400 × 75% (April 1998 to August 2003)	13,800
Taxable gain subject to annual exemption	£4,600

Notes

(a)   Taper relief on the deferred gain becoming chargeable is given by reference to the time and circumstances of the original disposal, not the disposal which brings the gain into charge. This applies in a number of circumstances in which gains are deferred or postponed, as listed at *TCGA 1992, Sch A1 para 16*. For a further example, see 209.3(A) ENTERPRISE INVESTMENT SCHEME.

(b)   A special rule applies in cases of serial EIS reinvestment. See 209.3(B) ENTERPRISE INVESTMENT SCHEME.

(c)   Deferral relief under *TCGA 1992, Sch 5C* is abolished for VCT shares issued after 5 April 2004. [*FA 2004, s 94, Sch 19 paras 4–7*].

229   Wasting Assets

Cross-references. See also 215.3 LAND, 224.3 ROLLOVER RELIEF—REPLACEMENT OF BUSINESS ASSETS.

229.1 **GENERAL** [*TCGA 1992, ss 44–47*]

V bought an aircraft on 31 May 2001 at a cost of £90,000 for use in his air charter business. It has been agreed that V's non-business use of the aircraft amounts to one-tenth, on a flying hours basis, and capital allowances and running costs have accordingly been restricted for income tax purposes. On 1 February 2007, V sells the aircraft for £185,000. The aircraft is agreed as having a useful life of 20 years at the date it was acquired.

		£
Amount qualifying for capital allowances		
Relevant portion of disposal consideration $\frac{9}{10} \times$ £185,000		166,500
Relevant portion of acquisition cost $\frac{9}{10} \times$ £90,000		81,000
Chargeable gain 2006/07 (subject to TAPER RELIEF (228))		£85,500
Amount not qualifying for capital allowances		
Relevant portion of disposal consideration $\frac{1}{10} \times$ £185,000		18,500
Relevant portion of acquisition cost		
$\frac{1}{10} \times$ £90,000	9,000	
Deduct Wasted £9,000 $\times \dfrac{\text{5y 8m}}{\text{20y}}$	2,550	6,450
Gain		£12,050

The whole of the £12,050 is exempt.

The total chargeable gain (subject to taper relief) is therefore £85,500

Note

(*a*)   Gains on tangible movable property which are wasting assets not qualifying for capital allowances are exempt (and any losses would not be allowable). [*TCGA 1992, s 45*].

229.2 **OPTIONS** [*TCGA 1992, ss 44, 46, 146*]

Cross-reference. See also 203.1 ASSETS.

(A) Unquoted shares
On 1 July 2004, R grants C an option to purchase unquoted shares held by R. The cost of the option is £600 to purchase 10,000 shares at £5 per share, the option to be exercised by 31 December 2006. On 1 September 2006 C assigns the option to W for £500.

	£	£
Disposal consideration		500
Acquisition cost	600	
Deduct Wasted £600 × $\frac{26}{30}$	520	80
Chargeable gain		£420

(B) Traded options
On 1 December 2006, C purchases 6-month options on T plc shares for £1,000. Two weeks later, he sells the options, which are quoted on the Stock Exchange, for £1,200.

	£
Disposal consideration	1,200
Allowable cost	1,000
Chargeable gain	£200

Note
(*a*)   The wasting asset rules do not apply to traded options. [*TCGA 1992, s 146*].

229.3 **LIFE INTERESTS** [*TCGA 1992, s 44(1)(d)*]

(A)
N is a beneficiary under a settlement. On 30 June 1992, when her actuarially estimated life expectancy was 40 years, she sold her life interest to an unrelated individual, R, for £50,000. N dies on 31 December 2006, and the life interest is extinguished.

R will have an allowable loss for 2006/07 as follows

	£	£
Disposal consideration on death of N		Nil
Allowable cost	50,000	
Deduct wasted		
$\frac{14y\ 6m}{40y} \times £50,000$	18,125	
		31,875
Allowable loss		£31,875

Note
(*a*)   The amount of the cost wasted is computed by reference to the predictable life, not the actual life, of the wasting asset.

229.3 Wasting Assets

(B)

Assume the facts to be as in (A) above except that the sale of the life interest was on 30 June 1981 and N's life expectancy *at that date* was 40 years. The value of the life interest remained at £50,000 at 31 March 1982.

Calculation without re-basing

	£	£
Disposal consideration on death of N		Nil
Allowable cost	50,000	
Deduct wasted		
$\dfrac{25\text{y 6m}}{40} \times £50,000$	31,875	
	———	18,125
Loss		£18,125

Calculation with re-basing

	£	£
Disposal consideration		Nil
Market value 31.3.82	50,000	
Deduct wasted		
$£50,000 \times \dfrac{24\text{y 9m}\ (31.3.82-31.12.06)}{39\text{y 3m}\ \text{(life expectancy at 31.3.82)}}$	31,529	
	———	18,471
Loss		£18,471
Allowable loss 2005/06		£18,125

Note

(*a*) The second of the above calculations shows how the wasting assets provisions interact with the re-basing provisions of *TCGA 1992, s 35*. Where, by virtue of the re-basing rules, an asset is deemed to have been disposed of and re-acquired at its market value on 31 March 1982, that market value must be reduced in accordance with the period of ownership *after* that date and the predictable life of the wasting asset *at* that date.

Table of Statutes

1970 Taxes Management Act

s 59B(4)	214.1
s 59C	214.1
s 86	214.1
s 88	214.1(B)

1979 Capital Gains Tax Act

s 44	212.1(D)

1980 Finance Act

s 79	205.2; 211.1(C)

1984 Inheritance Tax Act

s 49A	225.6
s 49C	225.6
s 71A	225.6
s 71D	225.6
s 89B(1)	225.6

1988 Income and Corporation Taxes Act

s 34	215.3(C)
s 87	215.3(G)
s 122	218.1
s 247	202.3
s 249	226.7
s 251(2)–(4)	226.7
s 282A	217.2
s 282B	217.2
s 291	209.3(A)
s 291B	209.3(A)
s 312	209.3
(1A)(*a*)	209.1; 209.2(B)
(1)	201.1(A)
s 575	216.3
s 576	216.8
(4)–(4B)	216.3
s 686(1A)	225.1
s 740(6)	219.1(D)
Sch 18 para 1(5)	226.6

1988 Finance Act

s 34	217.2
ss 130–132	220.1

1991 Finance Act

s 72	201.1(A)

1992 Taxation of Chargeable Gains Act

s 2(2)	201.2; 219.1(A)
(4)–(8)	201.2; 216.2; 219.1(B)
s 2A	224.1(A)(C); 224.2(A); 228.1
(1)(2)	204.3(A)(B)(C)
(5)	228.2(B); 228.3
(6)	228.1(B)
(8)(9)	227.1; 228.2(B); 228.3(A)
s 3	201.2; 225.1
s 4	217.1
(1AA)	225.1
s 8(2)	207.1
s 10	220.3
ss 19, 20	202.4
s 22	206.3
(1)	206.1
s 23	206.3; 206.3(B)(C)
(1)	206.3(E)
(2)	206.3(D)
s 25	220.1; 220.3
(1)(3)(8)	220.3
s 29	202.1
s 30	202.2; 202.3
s 31	202.3
s 35	205.1; 215.3(E); 221.5; 229.3(B)
(1)	205.1(A)
(2)	204.1(A); 204.3(B); 205.1(A); 215.3(E)
(3)	204.3(C); 205.1(A); 208.2(A)
(*a*)	204.3(A)(B)(C); 215.3(E)
(*b*)	204.1(B); 204.3(D)
(*c*)	204.1(B); 205.1(B)
(*d*)	205.2; 212.2(A)
(4)	204.3(B); 205.1(A)
(5)	204.1(A); 205.1(A)(B); 208.2(B); 220.1
(7)	221.1
s 38	208.1(A); 211.1(B)
s 39	208.1(A); 215.3(G)
s 41	208.1(B); 220.2
s 42	204.3(E); 208.2; 215.3(B); 217.2; 226.3
(4)	208.2(A)
s 44	203.1; 229.1; 229.2
(1)(*d*)	229.3
s 45	229.1; 229.1(A)
s 46	203.1; 229.1; 229.2

Table of Statutes

1992 Taxation of Chargeable Gains Act

s 47	229.1
s 53	209.1(B); 212.1; 215.4
(1)	206.3(E)
(*b*)	212.1(D)
(1A)	206.3(E);
	209.1; 211.1(C); 212.1(B)
(2A)	212.1(D)
(3)	206.3(E); 215.2(B)
s 54	212.1
(1)	209.1
(1A)	209.1;
	211.1(C); 212.1(B)
(4)(*b*)	215.3(F)
s 55	212.1
(1)(2)	204.1(A);
	204.3(A)(C); 205.1(A);
	208.2(A); 212.1(C); 215.3(E);
	227.2
(5)(6)	212.2(A)(C)
(7)–(9)	212.2(C)
s 56	212.1
(2)	212.2(A)–(D)
(3)	212.2(D)
(4)	212.2(D)
s 57	206.3(E); 215.2(B)
s 58	212.2(A); 217.1; 217.1(B)
s 59	221.1
s 62	212.1(C)
s 67	211.1(C)
s 70	225.4
s 71	225.5
(2)–(2D)	225.5(B)
s 72	225.6
s 76	225.6(B)
s 77	201.2; 216.2;
	225.1; 225.2; 225.3; 225.4(B)
(2)–(5)	225.1
(6)	225.2
ss 78, 79	225.1;
	225.2; 225.3; 225.4(B)
s 86	201.2; 216.2
s 87	201.2; 219
s 89(2)	201.2; 219.1(A)
s 91(3)–(5)	219
ss 91–93	219
s 97	219
s 104	227.2
s 105	207.2;
	226.3(C); 227.1; 227.2
ss 105A, 105B	227.1
s 106	207.2
s 106A	223.1; 226.3(C); 227.1
s 107	227.2

s 108	227.2
(1)	223.1
s 109	227.2
(2)	226.3(C)
(4)	204.1; 204.1(A)
(5)	204.1
s 110	227.2
s 110A	226.2(A)(B);
	226.3(A); 227.1
s 115	223
s 116	223; 223.2
(10)	223.2
s 117	216.3; 223; 223.1
(1)	223.1; 226.6
(7)(*b*)(8)	223.1
s 119	212.3
s 122	226.4(A);
	226.8(A); 226.8(B)
(2)	226.8(B)
s 123	226.8(B)
(1)	226.3
s 126	226.1; 226.2
s 127	223.2;
	225.1; 226.1(A); 226.2;
	226.3(C); 226.4(A); 228.2
s 128	223.2; 226.1;
	226.2; 226.3(C); 226.7
(4)	226.3
s 129	223.2; 226.1; 226.1(A)
s 130	223.2; 226.1;
	226.1(B); 226.2
s 131	226.1
s 132	226.4(E); 226.6
s 135	226.4; 226.4(A)
s 136	226.5
s 137	226.4
s 138	226.4; 226.5
s 138A	226.4(E)
s 140	220.4
s 141	226.7
s 142	226.7
s 144	203.1
ss 144ZA–144ZD	203.1
s 145	203.1
s 146	229.2; 229.2(B)
s 150A(1)	209.2;
	209.3; 209.3(B)
(2)(2A)(3)	209.1; 209.2
s 150D	209.3(B)
s 152	207.2; 224; 224.1
(7)(9)	224.2(B)
s 153	224; 224.2(A)
s 154	224; 224.3
s 155	224

ss 156–158	224
s 162	211.3(A)(B)
s 162A	211.3(B)
s 164A	211.3
s 165	211.1(C); 211.2
(10)	211.1(C)
ss 169B–169G	211.1(A); 222.4; 225.4(A)
s 171	212.2(C)(D); 220.2
s 172	220.2
s 176	202.5
ss 185, 187	220.1
ss 201–203	218.1
s 222	222.1; 222.1(B)
(5)	222.2
s 223	222.1; 222.4
(1)	222.1(A)(B); 222.4
(2)	222.4
(3)(a)(b)	222.1(B)
(4)(7)	222.1(A)(B)
s 224(1)(2)	222.3
s 225	225.5(A)
ss 226A, 226B	222.4
s 242	208.2(D); 215.1
(2)	215.1
s 243	215.2; 215.2(B)
ss 244–246	215.2
s 247	215.2; 215.2(A)
s 248	215.2
s 260	211.1; 222.4; 225.4(A)(B)
(5)	211.1(B)
(7)	211.1(C)
s 262	202.4
(2)	210.1(A)
(3)	210.1(B)
(4)	210.1(C)
ss 279A–279D	216.4
s 283	213.1
Sch A1	228.1
para 3	228.2; 228.2(A)
4	228.2(B)
(2)	228.2(B)
6	228.2(B)
(1)	228.2(B)
(2)(3)	228.2(B)
9	222.3
13(3)	208.5
15	228.3
16	209.3(A); 222.2; 228.3
22(1)	228.2(B)
Sch 1 para 2	225.1

Sch 2 para 1	204.1
2	204.1
(1)	204.1(B)
3	204.1
4	204.1; 204.1(A)
5	204.1
6	204.1
paras 7, 8	204.1
9–15	204.2
para 16	204.3; 204.3(D)
(3)–(5)(8)	204.3(E)
paras 17, 18	204.3
para 19	204.3
(1)	204.3(C)
(2)	204.3(D)
(3)	204.3(C)(D)
Sch 3 para 1	212.2(A)
4(1)	204.3(E); 208.2(B); 226.4(A)
(2)	206.3(D)
6	204.3(B)
7	205.1(A)
paras 8, 9	205.1(A)
Sch 4	205.2; 211.3(A)
para 1(a)	205.2
2	205.2
4	222.2
paras 5–9	205.2
Sch 5B	209.3
Sch 5BA	209.3; 209.3(B)
Sch 5C	228.3
Sch 7	211.2
Sch 8 para 1	215.3 (A)(D)(E)(F)(G)
(2)	215.3(A)
(4)(b)	215.3(F)
2	215.3(B)(C)
4	215.3(H)(J)
5	215.3(C)(H)(J)
(2)	215.3(H)(J)
Sch 11 para 10(1)	202.2
(2)	202.3

1994 Finance Act

s 93(1)(2)	206.1(B);206.2(D); 207.1(B); 210.1(D)
(3)	209.1(B)

1995 Finance Act

ss 66, 67	209
Sch 13	209

1996 Finance Act

Sch 21 para 42(3)	204.3

Table of Statutes

1996 *Finance Act*
Sch 21 para 43 — 205.2

1997 **Finance Act**
s 89 — 226.4(E)
s 90 — 209.3

1998 **Finance Act**
s 121 — 203.1; 209.3(A)
(1) — 204.3(B)(C);
209.1; 224.1(A)(C);
224.2(A); 228.1(B); 228.2;
228.3; 228.3(A)
(2) — 209.1; 223.2
(3) — 209.1
(4) — 204.3(B)(C);
223.2; 227.1; 228.4
s 122(1) — 211.1(C); 221.1
(2) — 211.1(C)
(3) — 211.1(C)
(4) — 208.4(E); 221.1
s 124(1)(2)(7) — 227.1
s 125(2)(4)(5) — 226.2(A)(B);
226.3(A); 227.1
s 144 — 203.1
Sch 13 para 6 — 209.3
12 — 209.2(B)
paras 26–36 — 209.3;
203.1; 209.3; 222.2
Sch 20 — 209.3(A); 226.4
Sch 27 Part III(31) — 224

2000 **Finance Act**
s 37 — 201.1
s 63(2)(3) — 216.3
s 66 — 224.1(C);
224.2(A); 227.1; 228.1
(2) — 228.4
(3) — 228.2;
228.2(B); 228.3(A)
(4) — 228.2;
228.2(B); 228.3(A); 228.4
s 67 — 228.2(B)
(4) — 228.2(B)
(5) — 228.2(B)
(7) — 228.2(B)
Sch 16 para 3(3) — 216.3
Sch 17 para 6(4) — 209.1
7(2)(3) — 209.3
8 — 209.1; 209.3
Sch 29 para 3 — 220.2
12 — 208.2(B)
18 — 207.2

2001 **Capital Allowances Act**
Sch 2 para 78 — 208.2(B)

2001 **Finance Act**
s 78 — 229; 229.2(B)
Sch 15 para 10 — 209.3(A)
paras 25–37 — 209.3
para 38 — 216.3
40 — 209.3; 209.3(A)
Sch 26 — 228
para 3 — 228.2(B)

2002 **Finance Act**
s 45 — 226.4
s 46 — 206.3(E); 228.1; 228.2(B)
s 49 — 211.3(B)
s 50(1)(2) — 227.1
s 51 — 201.2; 216.2
s 84 — 211.3(A); 224.1(A)
Sch 9 para 1 — 226.4
2 — 226.5
7 — 226.4; 226.5
Sch 11 para 2 — 201.2; 216.2
3 — 216.2; 226.2
7 — 201.2; 216.2
8 — 201.2;
216.2; 225.2
Sch 29 — 211.2(B);
211.3(A); 224.1(A)
para 95 — 211.3(A)
paras 117, 118 — 211.3(A)
para 121 — 211.3(A)
132 — 211.1(A)
137 — 224.1(A)

2003 **Finance Act**
s 158 — 203.1
s 160 — 228.1; 228.2(B)
s 161 — 226.4(C)
s 162 — 216.4

2004 **Finance Act**
s 94 — 228.4
s 116 — 211.1(A)
s 117 — 222.4
Sch 19 paras 4–7 — 228.4
Sch 21 — 211.1(A)
Sch 22 paras 6–8 — 222.4

2005 **Income Tax (Trading and Other Income) Act**
ss 60–63 — 215.3(G)
s 64 — 215.3(G)
ss 65–67 — 215.3(G)

s 157	218.1	**2006 Finance Act**	
s 277	215.3(C)	s 69	207.1
ss 278–281	215.3(C)	s 72(1)(3)	207.2
s 319	218.1	s 74	227.1
ss 340–343	218.1	Sch 12 paras 3, 13	225.2
Sch 1 para 106	218.1	para 28	225.1
451	215.3(C)	para 1	225.2
(2)	215.3(J)	30	225.6
		33	225.2
		paras 34, 36	219.1(A)
2005 Finance Act		para 38	225.1
ss 23–45	225.3	41	219.1(A)
Sch 1	225.3	44	225.1
		48	225.2
2005 Finance (No 2) Act		Sch 13 para 35	225.2
s 35	203.1	Sch 20 para 30	225.6
Sch 5 paras 1, 2, 6	203.1	Sch 26 Pt 3(10)	207.2

Index

This index is referenced to chapter and paragraph number within the book. The entries in bold capitals are chapter headings in the text.

A

Accrued income scheme
CGT effect   211.3; 223.1
Allowable and non-allowable
  expenditure   **208.1**
ANNUAL RATES AND
  EXEMPTIONS   **201**
losses, interaction with   201.2
—attributed settlement
  gains   201.2(B)
married persons   217.1
settlements   225.1
ANTI-AVOIDANCE   **202**
disposal to connected person   202.4
gains of offshore settlements   219.1
groups of companies
—depreciatory transactions   202.5
value-shifting   202.1; 202.2; 202.3
ASSETS   **203**
options   203.1; 229.2
Assets disposed of in series of
  transactions   **202.4**
ASSETS HELD ON 6 APRIL
  1965   **204**
buildings   204.3(B)
chattels   204.3(A)
land and buildings   204.3(B)
land reflecting development
  value   204.2
part disposals after
  5 April 1965   204.3(F)
quoted shares and securities   204.1
time apportionment   204.3
unquoted shares   204.3(C)(D)(E)
ASSETS HELD ON
  31 MARCH 1982   **205**
deferred gains, relief for   205.2
general computation of
  gains/losses   205.1
no gain/no loss
  disposals   212.2(A)(C)
part disposals before
  6 April 1988   208.2(B)
partnerships, held by   221.1
private residences   222.1(A)(B)
short leases   215.3(E)

wasting assets   229.3(B)

B

Bondwashing
CGT effect   223.1
Building Societies
conversions and takeovers   226.9
Business assets
deferment of chargeable gain on
  replacement of assets   224
gift of   211.2
taper relief   228.2(A)(B)
transfer to a company   211.3

C

Capital allowances
capital gains, effect on   208.1(B); 220.2; 229.1
Capital losses
See Losses
CAPITAL SUMS DERIVED FROM
  ASSETS   **206**
deferred consideration   206.2; 216.4; 226.4(C)
receipt of compensation   206.3; 215.2
—capital sum exceeding allowable
  expenditure   206.3(D)
—compulsory acquisition   215.2
—indexation allowance   206.3(E)
—part application of capital sum
  received   206.3(C)
—restoration using
  insurance moneys   206.3(B)
Chattels   **210.1**
held on 6.4.65   204.3(A)
CIVIL PARTNERS
See also Married Persons and Civil
  Partners
transfers between   212.1(D); 212.2(A); 217.1; 217.2; 228.3
COMPANIES   **207**
capital losses   207.1
exchange of securities   226.4
reconstruction schemes   226.5
shares — acquisitions and disposals
  within short period   207.2

transfer of assets to non-resident
company 220.3
Companies (migration of) **220.1**
Compensation
CGT on receipt of 206.3; 215.2
—taper relief 206.3(E)
Compulsory acquisition of
land **215.2**
COMPUTATION OF GAINS AND
LOSSES **208**
allowable expenditure 208.1
—effect of capital
allowances 208.1(B)
compulsory acquisition
of land 215.2
connected persons 202.4
part disposal 206.1(A);208.2;
206.3(A); 214.1; 215.2; 217.2
—assets held on 6.4.65 204.3(E)
—small part disposals of land 215.1
premiums payable under leases 215.3
sets, assets forming 202.4
value passing out of shares 202.1;
202.2; 202.3

Corporate bonds,
qualifying **223; 226.6**

D

Deferment of chargeable gain
See Hold-over reliefs and Rollover relief
Deferred consideration **206.1(B);**
216.4; 226.4(C)
Depreciatory transactions **202.5**
Dwelling house, gains on **222**

E

Earn-outs **216.4; 226.4(C)**
ENTERPRISE INVESTMENT
SCHEME **209**
capital gains and losses
—disposal more than three years after
acquisition 209.1; 209.2
deferral relief 209.3
—serial investors 209.3(B)
EXEMPTIONS AND
RELIEFS **210**
chattels 210.1
dwelling house 222
qualifying corporate bonds 223
tangible movable asset 210.1

G

Gifts **211**
assets held on 31 March 1982 206.2
business assets 211.2
deferment of gain 211.1;
211.2; 224.3
Groups of companies
depreciatory transactions 202.5
distribution followed by disposal of
shares 202.3
intra-group transfers
of assets 212.2(C)(D)

H

HOLD-OVER RELIEFS **211**
See also Rollover Relief
assets held on 31 March 1982 205.2
chargeable lifetime
transfers 211.1(A)
disposal consideration 211.1(B)
gifts
—business assets 211.2
—chargeable lifetime
transfers 211.1
IHT relief 211.1(C)
private residences and 222.4
transfer of business to
company 211.3
—election to disapply
relief 211.3(B)
—incorporation relief 211.3(A)
Husband and wife
See Married Persons

I

Incorporation relief **211.3; 211.3(A)**
election to disapply 211.3(B)
INDEXATION **212**
allowance on receipt of
compensation 206.3(E)
assets held on 31.3.82 212.1(C)
general rules 212.1
indexation factor, calculation of
—companies 212.1(A)
—individuals, etc. 212.1(B)
no gain/no loss
disposals 212.2(A)–(D)
—intra-group transfers 212.2(C)(D)
—transfers between spouses or civil
partners 212.2(A)(B)
restriction 212.1(D)

Index

shares and securities,
  identification rules   227.2
Inter-spouse transfers   **212.1(D);**
     212.2(A); 217.1; 217.2; 228.3
taper relief   228.3
Interest in possession
  termination of   225.5; 225.6
INTEREST ON OVERPAID
TAX   **213**
INTEREST ON UNPAID TAX   **214**

L

LAND   **215**
  compulsory purchase   215.2
  development value,
    reflecting   204.2
  held on 6.4.65   204.2; 204.3(B)
  leases   215.3
  —assignment of
    short lease   215.3(D)–(G)
  —grant of long lease   215.3(B)
  —grant of short lease   215.3(C)
  —premiums on short
    leases   215.3(C)(G)(H)(J)
  —short leases which are not wasting
    assets   215.3(A)
  —sub-lease granted
    out of short lease   215.3(H)(J)
  small part disposals   215.1
Leases
  See Land
LOSSES   **216**
  capital losses   207.1; 214
  —election to treat as arising in earlier
    year   216.4
  —indexation losses   212.1(D)
  —set-off against settlement
    gains   216.2
  —tangible movable
    assets   210.1(B)
  chattels   210.1(B)
  interaction with annual
    exempt amount   201.2
  rights to unascertainable
    consideration   216.4
  unlisted companies   216.3
  unquoted shares, capital losses available
    for set-off against income   216.3

M

MARRIED PERSONS AND CIVIL
  PARTNERS   **217**

jointly owned assets   217.2
no gain/no loss
  transfers   212.2(A)(B);
     217.1; 217.2
taper relief   228.3
Migration of companies   **220.1**
MINERAL ROYALTIES   **218**

N

Non-resident, company
  becoming   **220.1**
Non-resident company, transfer
  of assets to   **220.3**
Non-residents trading through UK
  permanent establishment   **220.2**

O

OFFSHORE SETTLEMENTS   **219**
  gains attributed to UK
    beneficiary   219.1
Options   **203.1; 229.2**
Overdue tax
  See Interest on Unpaid Tax
OVERSEAS MATTERS   **220**
  See also Offshore Settlements
  company migration   220.1
  non-residents trading through
    UK branch or agency   220.2
  overseas resident settlements   219
  transfer of assets to non-resident
    company   220.3
  UK beneficiary of an overseas resident
    settlement   219.1

P

Part disposals
  See Disposal
PARTNERSHIPS   **221**
  accounting adjustments   221.3
  assets   221.1
  —distribution in kind   221.6
  changes in partners   221.2–221.4
  changes in sharing ratios   221.2–221.5
  consideration outside
    accounts   221.4
  disposal of partnership asset
    to partner   221.6
  indexation   212.2(A)(C); 221.2
  revaluation of assets   221.3; 221.5
  shares acquired in stages   221.5
Permanent establishment   **220.2**

PRIVATE RESIDENCES   **222**
capital gains tax exemption   222
—hold-over relief obtained on earlier
    disposal   222.4
—part business use   222.3

Q

**QUALIFYING CORPORATE
   BONDS**   **223**
conversion of securities   226.6
definition   223.1
reorganisation of share
    capital   223.2

R

**Repayments of tax,
   interest on**   **213.1**
Residence and domicile
non-resident company, transfer
    of assets to   220.2
offshore settlements   219.1
ROLLOVER RELIEF   **224**
compulsory acquisition of
    land   215.2
gifts   205.2; 211.1; 211.2; 225.4
receipt of compensation not treated as
    disposal   206.3(B)–(E); 215.2
replacement of business assets   224
—nature of relief   224.1
—partial relief   224.2
—taper relief   224.1(C)
—wasting assets   224.3
transfer of business to a
    company   211.3
Royalties
mineral royalties   218

S

Securities
See Shares and Securities
SETTLEMENTS   **225**
annual exemptions   225.1
attributed gains, set-off of personal
    losses against   216.2
creation of   225.4
death of life tenant   225.6; 229.3
interest in possession   225.6
offshore   219.1
person becoming absolutely entitled
    to settled property   225.5
rates of tax   225.1

settlor retaining an interest   225.2
termination of an interest in
    possession   225.5
vulnerable beneficiary, with   225.3
**Settlements with interests in
   possession**   **225.6**
termination of an interest in
    possession   225.5
—losses   225.6(C)
SHARES AND SECURITIES   **227**
acquisitions and disposals within short
    period   207.2
bonus issues   226.2
capital distributions   226.8
conversion of securities   226.6
corporate bonds, qualifying   223
deferred consideration   206.2;
                  216.4; 226.4(C)
earn-outs   216.4; 226.4(C)
exchange of securities   226.4
holdings at 6.4.65
—quoted   206.1
—unquoted   206.3(C)(D)
qualifying corporate bonds   223
reconstruction schemes   226.5
reorganisation of share
    capital   223.2; 226.1
rights issues   226.1; 226.3
—sale of rights   226.8(B)
scrip dividends   226.7
time apportionment
—unquoted shares   204.3(D)
transfer of business to a company for
    shares   211.3
unquoted shares
—losses relieved against income   216.3
—time apportionment   204.3(D)
value passing out of   202.1;
                  202.2; 202.3
**SHARES AND SECURITIES—
   IDENTIFICATION RULES**   **227**
after 5 April 1998   227.1
companies   227.2
qualifying corporate bonds   223.1

T

Tangible movable property   **210.1**
TAPER RELIEF   **228**
basic rules   228.1(A)
business assets, part use as   228.2
compensation   206.3(E)
EIS deferral, interaction
    with   209.3(B)

Index

FA 2000 changes   CTG 229.2(B)
losses   228.1(B)
postponed gains   228.3
rollover relief, interaction
   with   228.1(C)
transfers between spouses or civil
   partners   228.3
Time apportionment   **204.3**
**Transfer of business to a
   company**   **211.3**
Trusts
   See Settlements

V

Value-shifting
   anti-avoidance   202.1; 202.2; 202.3

Vulnerable beneficiary
   trusts with   225.3

W

WASTING ASSETS   **229**
   eligible for capital
     allowances   229.1
   —assignment of short
     lease   215.3(D)–(G)
   —grant of long lease   215.3(B)
   —grant of short lease   215.3(C)
   —short leases which are not wasting
     assets   215.3(A)
   —sub-lease granted out of short
     lease   215.3(H)(J)
   life interests   229.3
   options   203.1; 229.2
   rollover relief   225.4